Java™ 2 Performance and Idiom Guide

Craig Larman
Rhett Guthrie

Prentice Hall PTR
Upper Saddle River, NJ 07458
http://www.phptr.com

ISBN 0-13-014260-3

90000

9 780130 142603

Editorial/Production Supervision: Kerry Reardon
Editor-in-Chief: Jeff Pepper
Editorial Assistant: Linda Ramagnano
Manufacturing Manager: Alexis Heydt
Marketing Manager: Dan Rush
Cover Designer: Craig Larman
Cover Production: Talar Agasyan
Cover Design Director: Jerry Votta

Prentice Hall books are widely used by corporation and government agencies for training, marketing, and resale.
The publisher offers discounts on this book when ordered in bulk quantities.
For more information, contact

   Corporate Sales Department,
   Prentice Hall PTR
   One Lake Street
   Upper Saddle River, NJ 07458
   Phone: 800-382-3419; FAX: 201-236-7141
   E-mail (Internet): corpsales@prenhall.com

Printed in the United States of America

10   9   8   7   6   5   4   3   2   1

ISBN 0-13-014260-3

Prentice-Hall International (UK) Limited, *London*
Prentice-Hall of Australia Pty. Limited, *Sydney*
Prentice-Hall Canada Inc., *Toronto*
Prentice-Hall Hispanoamericana, S.A., *Mexico*
Prentice-Hall of India Private Limited, *New Delhi*
Prentice-Hall of Japan, Inc., *Tokyo*
Prentice-Hall of Asia Pte. Ltd., *Singapore*
Editora Prentice-Hall do Brasil, Ltda., *Rio de Janeiro*

For Julie, Haley, and Hannah

With all my love and thanks for your support!

For Wendy

For always pushing me to be my best.

OVERVIEW

TABLE OF CONTENTS

2   IMPROVING PERFORMANCE—MODERATE-MINOR   61

3   IMPROVING PERFORMANCE—MINOR   93

PREFACE

Thank you for considering this book. We work in the roles of teacher and mentor to software developers relatively new to Java, and also as designers and developers ourselves. As such, we know that the material in this book is of real value to our students, and would have been appreciated by ourselves, if it had been available to us when we were starting out.

OBJECTIVES

The goal of this book is—for software developers fairly new to Java—to accelerate their mastery of some useful but slightly non-obvious common idioms that experienced Java developers apply, and to hasten their ability to design and implement faster Java applications.

In short, *Fast Java Fast*.

JAVA IDIOMS

As teachers, we wish to help accelerate our students' mastery of Java by sharing with them the *useful but somewhat non-obvious* "tricks of the Java trade" and the idioms that experienced Java developers apply.

For example:

- *java.lang.Constructor* objects can be used to create flexible *Factory* objects. A Java novice does not usually recognize this usage.

- The definition of *interfaces* does not self-evidently reveal that they are idiomatically used to group together constants shared by a package (or subsystem) into an interface with variables, but no operations.

This book collects together many such language and library idioms, so that you may more quickly gain mastery of effective Java.

In addition to language and library idioms, there are some common Java "idioms" in packaging, testing, and naming; idioms in the sense that they are moderately common practices. We wished to consolidate and share these to hasten the use of these broader Java-related skills for those relatively new to Java.

INTENDED AUDIENCE AND PREREQUISITES

Of course, the degree to which a Java idiom is "somewhat non-obvious" is a function of your familiarity with Java. Our intended audience is software engineers who have been recently introduced to Java, have a basic understanding of the language and libraries, and are ready for the next step: A deeper insight into how experienced developers use common language and library features in Java, and how to design Java systems with adequate performance.

Little or no attempt is made to define basic Java features. For example, we assume you understand what an *inner class* is, and instead focus on how inner classes are idiomatically used.

JAVA PERFORMANCE

Performance is of concern to many of our students and to Java developers in general. Therefore, we wanted to collect an introduction to many general and Java-specific performance tips in one book, in order to shorten the learning cycle for you. Those fairly new to Java should find a variety of useful strategies, and although the experienced battle-scarred Java developer may be familiar with some of these performance tips, we hope they too will find a few new points of value.

SCOPE

With respect to performance strategies, the book presents a broad introduction to the subject. With respect to language idioms, we have been able to cover most of the common idioms related to syntax and keywords. On the other hand, the complete Java API is quite large, especially when you include the Enterprise APIs. Therefore, we decided to focus on the most widely used APIs, such as *java.lang*, *java.util*, and so forth. Although Swing is an important and widely used API, the subject is vast, the library is young, and we are not experts, so we decided to bypass it.

ACKNOWLEDGMENTS

Many thanks to all the reviewers. Our most diligent reviewer was Bernard Horan of Sun, who gets our very special thanks.

At Sun, thanks to Laura Hill for helping us connect with more reviewers. Thanks to Steve Wilson on the HotSpot team, who reviewed a draft of the performance chapters, while himself starting to write a new book on Java performance; we look forward to seeing his work published. Thanks also to Aaron Hughes and Chris Ferris.

This book would not have been possible without the experience of working at ObjectSpace, and the many wonderful people who have been our colleagues. Thanks to all the ObjectSpace reviewers and tip providers: Francis Anderson, Walter Bodwell, Jonathan Brumley, Ken Delong, Todd Girvin, Lois Goldthwaite, David Howard, Paul Jakubik, Chris Jones, Sonny Lacey, Toivo Lainevool, John Lammers, Thomas Liou, Paul McGuire, Laurel Neustadter, David Nunn, Charley Rego, Bavesh Soni, Thomas Wheeler, and David Whitmore.

Finally, thanks to our editor, Jeffrey Pepper, for encouraging us to write.

ABOUT THE AUTHORS

Rhett Guthrie has been a professional Java developer since early 1996. His Java experience ranges from systems-level (as technical lead of ObjectSpace's *Voyager* Enterprise JavaBeans implementation) to applications-level (designing distributed Java applications). He has written articles for the trade magazines *Component Strategies* and *Java Developer's Journal* and has patents pending for two innovative Java technologies. Rhett is a Senior Technology Partner at Axys Solutions, LLC., where he specializes in architecting e-commerce systems using Java Enterprise APIs and Microsoft DNA technologies.

Rhett holds a B.Sc. and M.Sc. in mathematics. He can be reached at rhett@acm.org.

Craig Larman is the author of the popular college and industry text *Applying UML and Patterns: An Introduction to Object-Oriented Analysis and Design*, and is a regular speaker at conferences on the subjects of patterns, analysis and design, and distributed object systems design. He also writes the *Java and Modeling* column in *Java Report*. He works as a technical director, teacher, and mentor at ObjectSpace, a company specializing in distributed object technologies. He has been using object technologies since 1984 when he started developing knowledge systems on LISP machines. For well over a decade he has assisted others in developing object systems, and in learning object-oriented analysis and design, C++, Java, and Smalltalk.

Craig holds a B.Sc. and M.Sc. in computer science, with research emphasis in artificial intelligence, object-oriented knowledge representation, and case-based reasoning. He may be reached at clarman@acm.org.

TYPOGRAPHICAL CONVENTIONS

This is a **new term** in a sentence.

This is a *Type* or *method* name in a sentence, or something we wish to *emphasize*.

PRODUCTION NOTES

The manuscript of this book was created with Adobe FrameMaker. The drawings were done with Visio. The body font is Palatino (11 pt.), and the code font is Courier New (9 pt., bold).

1 IMPROVING PERFORMANCE— MAJOR-MODERATE

In this chapter

- Introduction to high-level, high-impact strategies to optimize speed and memory usage. Some strategies may have only moderate impact.

- Case studies of high-level design changes to improve performance.

The following three chapters are an *introduction* to strategies to improve the speed performance of an application. Also included are suggestions to improve space performance by reducing object creation (and subsequent reclamation), but these are primarily recommended in order to help speed up an application.

Most of the influential techniques are not specific to Java, since it is high-level changes in algorithms and data structures that usually have the most significant optimization impact. Consequently, many of the strategies recorded in this chapter are applicable across other programming languages.

The subsequent two chapters cover moderate and minor improvements, in which there is increased discussion of specific Java language and library usage.

1.1   Some Stories…

Rather than just starting off with a list of optimization techniques, we thought it might be interesting to first share some stories of real applications in which performance was improved. These case studies mostly illustrate high-level algorithmic design changes. Interestingly, each story illustrates variations on just a few high-level general principles.

Case Study 1: Reduce Object Creation

Application purpose/context: Generate reports against a database, with the aid of an intermediate middle-tier object-relational subsystem (ORS) that materialized the database rows into objects. The reporting subsystem reported from objects, not from raw database records.[1]

The ORS tier was general-purpose and supported transactional use in which "dirty" objects (modified by a client application) were written back (updated) to the database upon a commit operation.

Original design: In order to support the identification of "dirty" objects that needed to be written back on a commit operation, the following technique was used. When a row was first read and materialized into an object, a "pristine" copy of the object was saved in a cache. A working copy of the object was returned to a client. When a commit operation occurred, the working copies were compared against their pristine copies; if not identical, they were "dirty" and needed to be written back to the database.

Performance problem: Report generation caused many *thousands* of objects and their pristine copies to be loaded into a cache (for example, "Show me all employees

---

1. It would have been easier to use a commercial report writer that directly read from a database, but there were requirements that compelled this customized reporting system.

in the United States"). The massive number of cached pristine copies strained memory resources and required more object creation, dramatically slowing performance of the reports. The general-purpose ORS had not been designed with this high-volume read-only context in mind.

Final design: By profiling, the designer realized the essential problem was the many pristine copies. In the case of report writing the context is read-only and it is known that there is no need to cache pristine copies, since the objects will never become "dirty." Consequently, the *PristineCache* class was replaced by a *NullCache* that did not store objects, and the (few) necessary methods were overridden to prevent creating and saving pristine copies. Exploiting polymorphism, the *NullCache* could be easily introduced into the existing design without other changes. The major decrease in the number of in-memory objects and object creation led to a large improvement in reporting speed.

As an aside, the use of the *NullCache* object which is a "no-operation" object, is an example of the *Null Object* pattern [PLOP 1997], which allows us to insert polymorphic objects into an existing design that simply do no work in their methods, rather than having to hard-code special case logic tests for a "no-op" case.

Techniques used: The main optimization techniques used here were to *reduce object creation* and *exploit patterns in usage*. More domain specific, database access subsystems can be optimized in several ways when it is known that there is only read-only access.

CASE STUDY 2: BATCH WORK

Application purpose/context: A real-time paging system that receives paging messages and logs them to an object database (ODMS), before subsequent forwarding.

Original design: As each message comes in, it is written to the object database. Meanwhile, other processes and threads of execution in the overall system are making fine-grained modification to the state of objects in the ODMS.

Performance problem: For the chosen ODMS the overhead of starting and committing a transaction was quite high. This transaction overhead, applied to many fine-grained database transactions, was a major performance bottleneck.

Final design: Using the *Command* design pattern [GHJV 1995], each database change request was represented as an object; for example, *AddObjectCommand* and *ModifyObjectCommand*. Instances of these classes were buffered in a shared queue for processing. The design was changed so that a separate thread of execution would start one database transaction for a large set of these command objects, committing the transaction after the set was processed. This made a dramatic improvement in performance.

Techniques used: The main optimization technique used here was to *do more work in each step, when the overhead of each step is high*; that is, **batching** work.

CASE STUDY 3: EXPLOIT DATA PATTERNS AND INCREASE CACHING

Application purpose/context: Automatically generate Java class (bytecode) files that represent help information, from a set of RTF files.

Original design: In step one, a Java application read from a set of RTF files and output a set of Java source files. In step two, a Java compiler read these newly created source files and then generated a set of bytecode class files.

Performance problem: This multi-step process was relatively slow.

Final design: The designer analyzed the generated bytecodes and discovered that a major contiguous block was identical in all cases; only a small portion varied in each file. So the large, common bytecode section was hard-coded into a Java program and stored in a byte array. The new design read from the RTF files and internally constructed a byte stream containing the bytecodes for each Java class (using the hard-coded byte array). It then directly wrote out the class files, bypassing the Java compiler step.

Techniques used: The main enabling optimization techniques used here were to *exploit patterns in the data* and to *cache reusable things*—in this case, the large common set of bytecodes. These techniques enabled the designer to avoid some (slow) intermediate file I/O and to bypass the slow step of invoking the Java compiler.

CASE STUDY 4: MOVE PROCESSING TO THE NODE WITH THE RESOURCES

This is another example of the same application described in a previous case study.

Application purpose/context: To generate reports against a database, with the aid of an intermediate middle-tier object-relational subsystem (ORS) that materialized the database rows into objects. The reporting subsystem reported from objects, not from raw database records.

Original design: The ORS was not on the same computer as the relational database.

Performance problem: The remote communication overhead of transferring large volumes of data between computer nodes.

Final design: The ORS was placed on the same computer as the relational database. There was a significant increase in performance.

Techniques used: The main optimization technique used here was to *move processing onto the node that has the required resources*.

In addition to the above, several relational databases now include a built-in Java Virtual Machine (JVM), so that we can deploy Java data processing applications directly inside of the database server (using JDBC). This is highly recommended.

Case Study 5: Use Large-Grained Remote Communication

Application purpose/context: Display monitoring information about a RAID disk configuration, and provide management services.

Original design: The system is composed of many compute nodes, with a JVM on each node. At each node are various physical devices that require monitoring from a centralized monitoring station. Each physical device had an associated Java instance (a "device proxy" object) that knows its state, and each of these Java instances was a remote object. A separate monitoring station displayed (in a Java GUI) the state of all devices, in a *JTable* view. Each row in the *JTable* represented a different device instance, and thus each row was associated with a different remote Java object.

Performance problem: The *JTable* at the monitoring station displayed on average 500 devices, each with 10 attributes (columns in the *JTable*). Thus, since each row was a Java remote object, it required 5,000 remote method invocations (500 remote objects x 10 property remote method calls) to fill the table for display. The overhead of the massive fine-grained remote object communication made the presentation of data far too slow.

Final design: The hundreds of Java device proxy objects were changed to being simple local objects—no longer remote-enabled. Instead, at each JVM, a remote-enabled *Facade* object was added that collected all the local information on the devices, by sending local messages to the device proxy objects. A single remote method call to the Facade object from the monitoring application resulted in a serialized collection of all the data for that node to be returned, and displayed. Performance was dramatically improved.

Techniques used: The main optimization technique used here was to *use large-grained remote communication*, which is a specialization of *do more work in each step, when the overhead of each step is high*. Network communication makes remote collaboration much slower than local collaboration, thus the need to do more in each remote call.

CASE STUDY 6: ADD MEMORY AND TUNE JVM SETTINGS

Application purpose/context: Record hotel reservations and manage hotel client information.

Original design: A client-server design in which Java clients (a Java application) collaborate with Enterprise JavaBeans server objects.

Performance problem: Response time on the client was slow, even for local operations.

Final design: No change was made to the design or code. Simply, 64 MB of memory was added to each client node, and the initial heap size for the JVM was increased to 32 MB (from a default of 1 MB). Performance noticeably improved.

Techniques used: The main optimization techniques used here were to *use faster hardware and more memory*, and *tune the JVM launcher options*. This illustrates the value of starting with easy changes.

1.2 PERFORMANCE AND THE DEVELOPMENT PROCESS

At what point in application development should we consider performance? A classic admonition promotes the following strategy: "make it run, make it right, make it fast." And the influential computer scientist Donald Knuth quipped that "...premature optimization is the root of all evil."

As an overarching goal, in most applications it is of primary importance to design such that there is a clean separation of concerns and so that the design is tuned for ease of adaptability and maintenance. Where possible, strive to separate interfaces and abstractions from implementations, so that better performing components can be plugged in with little or no impact to the existing architecture.

Nonetheless, although the point is well taken that we can get bogged down in early optimizations that obfuscate the code or design at great expense but with little benefit, we have seen too many development projects take a cavalier approach to performance until too late in the game. This has led to costly, massive rework and in some cases even to project failure.

Like most things in life, a happy medium is the solution. Practically speaking, we recommend the adoption of an iterative and incremental development process in which performance evaluation is included in early development cycles—but not the very earliest. In this approach development is broken down into many short cycles of, for example, four-week periods. Within each four-week cycle a small portion of the requirements is tackled—proceeding through analysis, design, programming, and testing. Each subsequent cycle may tackle a new portion of the requirements and thus the system grows in small increments (see [Larman 1997] for an elaboration). Rather than address new requirements, some development cycles may be devoted to refinement; that is, polishing the system with respect to performance, usability, adaptability, and so on.

So for example, the first and second four-week development cycles can be devoted to making a fundamental portion of the requirements simply work correctly—without special consideration to performance, except for following the usual overarching strategies such as reducing short-lived object creation. Then, after there is a small meaningful code base and a stable emerging design to evaluate for performance, the third four-week cycle (or perhaps a shorter two-week cycle) may be solely dedicated to polishing, *realistic* load testing (for examples, large transaction or data volume; many concurrent clients), profiling, identification of the performance bottlenecks, optimization, and redesign.[1] The fourth and fifth development cycles may again be dedicated to tackling new requirements, and so on. Over time

---

1. Early realistic load testing is seldom done. Consequently, inability to handle the real load is a common failure of new production systems.

more attention can be given to requirements and less to performance. If we consider performance in this balanced manner fairly early in the project lifecycle, then the application is more likely to scale up to meet the performance requirements without requiring massive rework at a late stage.

This schedule is meant to be suggestive rather than prescriptive. The point is that deferring performance profiling and re-design until the mid or late stages of a project is, in our observation, often very painful and costly.

One justifiable reason to defer performance considerations until later in the project lifecycle is if most of the development team is new to many of the project technologies. For example, a team that is brand new to Java already has enough on their plate—worrying about performance would overwhelm them. In that case, regular design and code reviews with someone proficient in Java performance issues will help avoid "a world of hurt." Another justifiable reason to ignore performance is when creating throw-away proof-of-concept applications.

What is meant by good performance? It is a relative, fuzzy term, that must ultimately be defined by the customer who is willing to pay for its achievement. We recommend writing a contract with the project stakeholders that quantifies the performance criteria; once it's met, stop fine-tuning. See the performance process patterns *Performance Criteria*, *Threshold Switch*, and *Performance Measurement* in [PLOP 1997] for a simple approach to writing and living up to a performance contract that is agreed to by all stakeholders.

1.3 PROFILING

An important step to optimizing is to use a profiler to identify the performance hot spots, otherwise time will be wasted optimizing sections of code that do not have a significant impact on performance.

JVMs include a command-line option to generate raw, text-oriented profiling information, but it is easier to use a commercial profiling tool that provides a graphical display, summarization reports, and drill-down reports of instance creation and time spent in methods—such as *OptimizeIt* or *JProbe*.

In essence, these tools provide reports that summarize instance creation (how many instances, and where they were created), and time spent in methods, sorted from high to low (see Figure 1.1 and Figure 1.2). The basic strategy is to focus on the high frequency areas of the reports, navigating into sub-reports that provide a breakdown of the information.

If the hot spot is in JDK library code or native methods, our options are fairly limited, such as caching the results, calling an alternative service, or replacing it. If the hot spot is in our code, a wide variety of the strategies discussed here can be applied.

When looking at the number of instantiations of a particular class, the most important statistic is if they are long-lived or short-lived objects. Focus performance tuning on reducing the creation of many short-lived objects, which affects performance via overactive garbage collection.

Figure 1.1 Sample memory profiler results. Focus on *String* and *ZipEntry*.

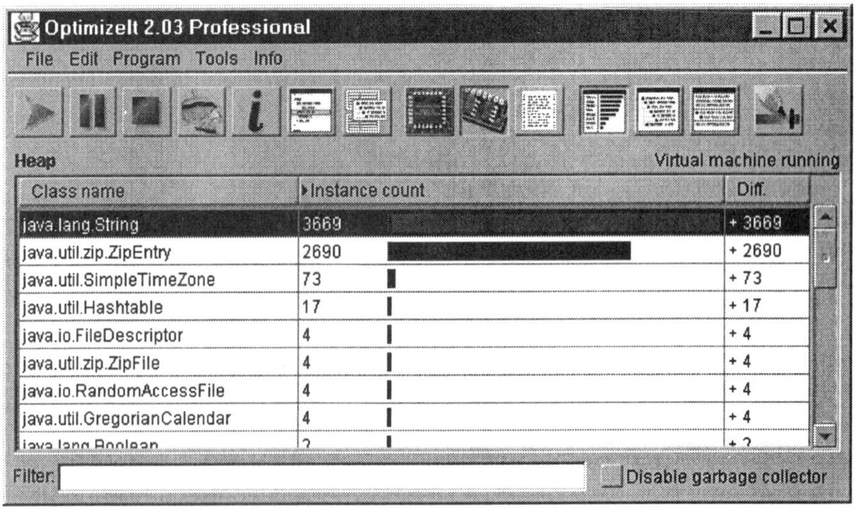

Figure 1.2 Sample CPU profiler results. Focus on highlighted area.

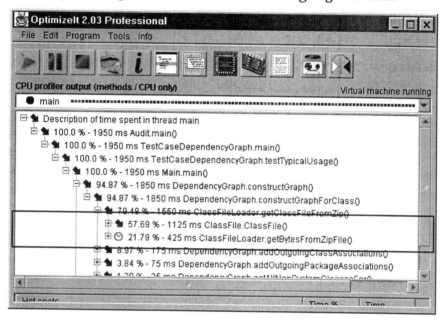

1.4   Introduction to the Strategies

We recommend starting with optimizing strategies that don't require changing the design or source code, such as adding more memory, increasing the initial heap size, and using a faster JVM. Using these strategies, we have seen performance improvements that range from the dramatic down to the trivial. If you're lucky, something as simple as adding another 64 MB of RAM and increasing the initial heap size will have a profound impact on the speed of your application. If you're not lucky, which is more likely the case, you'll have to move on to the other strategies described in these chapters—those that require changing the code.

With respect to design changes, the 80-20 rule[1] most definitely applies to optimization—in fact, it is more like 95-5. That is to say, there is usually only a critical five percent of the application that has the performance "hot spots"; improving performance in the other ninety-five percent makes no appreciable difference, because it is seldom executed or already performs well.

Hot spots come in two major varieties: (1) excessive instance creation, particularly of short-lived objects, and (2) methods in which the majority of time is spent.

Once we have identified the hot spots, we need to prioritize our optimization strategies. The strategies in this book are organized into high impact, moderate, and minor techniques. Of course, start with the most influential strategies—those described in this chapter, such as reducing object creation and increasing caching.

ORDER OF PERFORMANCE-RELATED ACTIVITIES

To summarize an appropriate order of activities related to performance:

1. First, write a performance contract with the stakeholders that defines the performance criteria. Obtain agreement that when met, optimization efforts can cease.

2. Design with abstractions and interfaces, so that implementations with different performance characteristics can be inserted with minimal impact.

3. From the beginning, design and program with consideration of easy, basic performance strategies that do not convolute the design, such as promoting inlined methods and reducing creation of many short-lived objects.

4. Apply strategies that do not require changing the source code, such as adjusting the initial heap size. These are the environment and tool strategies described ahead.

---

1. This rule has many variations, such as "20% of the code executes 80% of the time."

5. If performance criteria are not yet met, profile to identify the hot spots. Focus on methods that consume most of the processor time, and excessive short-lived object creation.

6. Most likely, the results of profiling will first suggest applying strategies to increase caching, reduce the excessive creation of short-lived objects, and doing more in one step, when the overhead of each step is high.

1.5 ENVIRONMENT AND TOOL STRATEGIES

These strategies do not require changing the design or Java source code, and are therefore worth trying first.

USE FASTER HARDWARE AND MORE MEMORY

What more can we say? (Well, lots actually, but we won't...)

USE THE SUN HOTSPOT JVM OR OTHER FAST JVM

An important milestone in the JVM performance wars was the release of version 1.0 of the HotSpot JVM for the Java 2 SDK. HotSpot offered significant performance improvements over prior Sun JVMs. Vigorous competition in the JVM market promises ongoing performance improvements both in HotSpot and competing JVMs from Microsoft, IBM, and others.

Although the following discussion focuses on HotSpot technology, as an example of a fast JVM of interest to many Java developers, we understand that this is an ever-shifting market. Evaluate the current best JVM for your application and platform by benchmarking some facsimile of your application with several JVMs.

Please note that we are not promoting HotSpot to the exclusion of other JVMs.

Note also that the first release of HotSpot was especially aimed at server-side Java, and Sun is releasing a client-side version optimized for typical client activities.

We are *not* enthusiastic about using benchmarks such as the SPECjvm for client-side JVM performance (available at www.spec.org) because these measure rather artificial isolated activities, such as mathematical operations, or repeated object creation in a tight loop. Such benchmarks don't capture the complex mix and interplay of operations in most real applications and are not reliable predictors of how your specific application will run on a JVM and platform. The adaptive compilation technology in HotSpot is a prime example related to this problem; it selectively optimizes the performance hot spots unique to an application while it is running. Thus, its performance benefits are seen when applied to *whole complex programs*. Therefore, benchmark the applications you care about.

To test the relative performance of HotSpot to its predecessor, we used a CPU-intensive and creation-intensive (non-GUI) Java application that analyzes the classes in a large JAR file, constructs an in-memory graph of nodes representing dependencies between the classes and packages (the graph is useful as input to a metrics analysis program), and writes a report to a text file.[1] Tests were run against *swingall.jar*, a relatively large collection of classes that implement Swing, the Java GUI framework.

---

1. This was a real Java application developed and used to solve a problem, not artificially constructed as a benchmark.

The results are shown in Figure 1.3.[1] Using HotSpot, the application ran in 65% of the time compared to the older just-in-time (JIT) JVM—a dramatic performance increase.

Other benchmarks and developers testing HotSpot report performance improvements ranging from negligible up to 300% over Sun's prior JIT JVM, which indicates that many variables affect the outcome. For example, HotSpot (and JIT JVMs) can't do anything about the speed of native libraries, so if an application is spending a significant amount of time in native libraries, no improvement will be seen. This is especially common with the old AWT, which relies on many native calls.

The test compares version 1.0 of the HotSpot JVM with the v1.2.1 SDK against the JIT JVM in the v1.2.0 SDK.

Figure 1.3 Our benchmark application runs significantly faster using HotSpot.

JVM Version	Average Time (milliseconds)
Sun Java 2 SDK v1.2.0 (JIT) JVM	7600
Sun Java 2 SDK v1.2.1 with HotSpot JVM v1.0. No incremental garbage collection (the default of HotSpot)	5000 (65% of 7600)
HotSpot with incremental garbage collection turned on.	7300 (96% of 7600)

---

1. Details of the hardware used in the test are not important; it is the relative change we wish to illustrate.

Tune the JVM Launcher Options

This results of tuning the JVM launcher options vary from dramatic to trivial. Of the options, increasing the initial *heap* size can be by far the most influential in improving performance. We know of one recent Java application that experienced approximately a 50% improvement in performance just by adding more physical memory, and increasing the value for the initial heap size. Conversely, other applications are not improved at all. In any event, it is easy to experiment.

The Memory Allocation Pool (Heap) Initial Size

The Java **memory allocation pool** or **heap** is the free space available for new objects. In HotSpot, the young object "nursery" and Old Object memory area can loosely be considered the heap. In HotSpot v1.0, the initial default heap size is 4 MB. If this is exhausted because the application is creating many or large objects, it can "grow" up to a maximum default of 64 MB.

Growing the heap is a relatively slow operation, probably requiring collaboration with the operating system to request more memory, and copying the old heap to the new larger heap. Consequently, if it is known that the heap size will need to be larger than 4 MB, performance will improve by specifying a larger initial size, equal to the maximum size actually required by the application.

In order to estimate the appropriate initial value, create a background thread that periodically checks the values from *Runtime.totalMemory* and *Runtime.freeMemory*. The numbers returned are approximate, but suitable to help estimate the parameter values when starting a JVM.

For HotSpot v1.0, the option to change the initial heap size is *-Xms*, and the maximum is changed with *-Xmx*. These are followed by either *<number>K* (kilobytes) or *<number>M* (megabytes). For example:

```
>java   -Xms32M  foo.Main
```

THREAD SCALING ON WINDOWS NT: REDUCE MEMORY RESERVATION PER NATIVE THREAD

The following recommendation only applies if:

1. You are running on Windows NT, and

2. your application needs to create thousands of threads, and

3. your JVM's default native stack reserve size is 1 MB or larger (different JVMs and versions vary on this value).

The Stack

In order to motivate the concluding advice, it is worthwhile first understanding stacks in Java. A **thread stack** is a data structure used to hold the parameters, local variables, and so on, for a single thread. There are two kinds of stacks in relation to Java:

1. A Java stack, which is internal to Java. One exists for each Java *Thread*.

2. A native thread stack, which exists for each native thread, which is associated with each Java *Thread*.

Within a thread, each call to another Java method adds another **stack frame** to the Java stack; the stack frame stores the parameters and local variables for one method invocation context. Exiting a method removes a frame from the stack.

If there were a logic bug in an application, and an infinite recursive call to a method occurred, then stack frame upon stack frame would be added to the Java stack, until the maximum space allocated for the stack was exhausted. This is a **stack overflow**, and will cause Java to throw a *StackOverflowError*, which is a Bad Thing.

The native stacks are only used when Java invokes native methods. For example, methods implemented in C or C++ use the native stacks. Stack overflows can also occur on the native stack due to logic bugs in native methods. A stack overflow could also occur (this is very rare) if the native method created many large objects as stack variables.

Loosely speaking, when a *Thread* object is started in Java, an associated native thread is allocated (for example, an NT thread), and an associated native thread stack is created. For each native thread stack, a certain amount of operating system (virtual) memory is initially reserved.

Now, here is the key point: On Windows NT, for some JVMs (or versions of a JVM), the default reserved memory for the stack for a native thread is 1 MB. Since there is a total of 2 GB of virtual memory allowed per process in NT, this limits the number of native threads per process to a theoretical maximum of 2048 (2048 MB / 1 MB), although in practice the limit is lower because of other limitations that the operating system places on the process.

It turns out that this default value of 1 MB is overly generous, and that 256 KB would have been adequate in most cases.

The reason this upper limit is a concern is that some Java applications, usually servers with a thread-per-request model, need to create many threads. Therefore, it is advantageous to tweak a JVM on NT to allow more native threads to be allocated, if the JVM is defaulting to 1 MB native stack reserves.

There may be one or two steps required to reduce the original native stack size reserve.

Step one is to invoke the JVM with a launcher option to specify the native stack size. The option to change the maximum native stack size is either -ss or -Xss, which is followed by either *<number>K* (kilobytes) or *<number>M* (megabytes). For example:

```
>java -Xss256K foo.Main
```

However, this value may be ignored if the JVM *executable* has a setting which is greater than 256 KB. NT executables have their own idea about what the native stack size should be, independent of the JVM launcher option value. It may be set to 256 KB, but some versions are set to 1 MB.

Therefore, to quadruple the number of threads that can be supported in NT we may need to reduce the native stack reserve to 256 KB instead of 1 MB. We can override the default initial native stack reserve value by tweaking the JVM executable, using the Microsoft Binary File Editor *editbin*[1]. For example, to set the initial native stack reserve to 256 KB:

```
>editbin /stack:262144 java.exe
```

Beware: This is a delicate reconfiguration, so test to ensure that there is adequate stack space.

CONSIDER A NATIVE COMPILER

As the use of Java matures and spreads, it is increasingly being used to create server-side applications or single platform applications, rather than applets. Consequently, the use of a static, native machine code compiler is both viable and *possibly* desirable, as it *may* improve performance. Several Java development environments now include a native compiler, and one can also purchase stand-alone native compilers that promise superior results to their IDE-bundled counterparts, such as the TowerJ native compiler.

A caveat is in order with respect to native compilers—there is significant variation in the speed of the executables they generate. For example, we native compiled the benchmarking application mentioned previously that was used to benchmark HotSpot—it generates a dependency graph between Java classes and packages. We used two native compilers: Symantec Cafe 3.0 native compiler, and the Tower TowerJ 2.2.7 native compiler.

As before with the HotSpot evaluation, we applied the native application to analyze *swingall.jar*. Note that neither native executable was as fast as simply running the application using HotSpot v1.0, which was a surprise to us (Figure 1.4).[2]

---

1. See http://www.javaworld.com/javaworld/jw-03-1999/jw-03-volanomark.html.
2. The details of the hardware are not important, it is the relative performance we wish to illustrate.

We understand that these benchmarks will be quickly dated. The point is not to make decisions based upon these particular results, but to note that the results are not what might have been expected, and that careful scrutiny of the latest JVMs and native compilers is most definitely called for.

Although HotSpot did very well in this case, some TowerJ customers have reported performance increases five and ten times faster than using a JVM. We are not claiming that JIT JVMs or HotSpot will be faster than native compiled applications in general. In addition, native compilers for Java are still immature, and are bound to improve significantly over the coming years. It will be very interesting to see how the performance battles between very fast JVMs like HotSpot and native compilers play out.

Figure 1.4 HotSpot application ran faster than native Win32 compiled versions.

Application Version	Average Time (milliseconds)
Native Win32 compiled executable using Symantec Cafe 3.0	26420
Native Win32 compiled executable using Tower TowerJ 2.2.7	13180
Sun HotSpot v1.0	5000

FOR SERVER-SIDE JAVA, EVALUATE PLATFORMS

For a server-side Java application, evaluating a Java platform requires considering both the raw execution speed of applications, and the scalability of the platform as more socket connections and threads are added. The **VolanoMark** is a popular server benchmark of Java platform scalability, which measures throughput of messages per second (see www.volano.com). Specifically, it is measuring how performance changes as socket connections and threads are added to the server, as more and more concurrent client connections are established. This is *not* the same as evaluating raw execution speed of a Java application running on a client machine, with only a few threads.

We understand that the following benchmark values from March 1999 will become quickly dated. They are not presented to base a recommendation upon, but rather to illustrate that the benchmark shows marked differences in platform scalability, and therefore, that viewing the latest version of the benchmark is worthwhile.

Figure 1.5 illustrates the best choices for server-side scalability follow (higher scores are better) as of March 1999. This benchmark was run with 2,100 concurrent socket connections (and related threads), all tests running on identical hardware.[1]

Figure 1.5 VolanoMark benchmark for server scalability.

Java Platform	Operating System	Score for 2,100 Connections
Sun JDK 2 v1.2.0	Solaris 7 for Intel	1183
Sun JDK 2 v1.2.0	Windows NT 4.0	622
IBM JDK 1.1.7 for Windows	Windows NT 4.0	498
Microsoft SDK 3.1	Windows NT 4.0	459

Comments:

- Many Java platforms would not run for 2,100 connections (either simply failing or thrashing), these four are the only ones that made the cut.

- At the time of this benchmark test, the Sun JDK on Solaris was the clear winner. Not only did the Sun JDK for Solaris have the best score, but it also scaled with the least degradation. There was only a 23% drop in performance from 300 to 2,100 connections.

---

1. As before, the specific hardware is not central to the benchmark. We only wish to draw attention to the significant relative performance results.

- The Sun and Microsoft JVMs for NT required special tweaking, to change the size of the native stack reserve per thread (see the related performance tip for details).

At a much lighter load of 300 connections, the four best performers changed. However, all scores are so similar that the four best performers could roughly be considered equivalent:

Java Platform	Operating System	Score for 300 Connections
IBM JDK 1.1.7 for Windows	Windows NT 4.0	2531
Novell JDK 1.1.5	Netware 5	2487
Microsoft SDK 3.1	Windows NT 4.0	2409
Sun JDK 2 v1.2.0	Windows NT 4.0	2381

MOVE PROCESSING ONTO THE COMPUTER THAT HAS THE REQUIRED RESOURCES

Remote object communication has a high gee-whiz factor, and multi-tiered physically distributed architectures look wonderful on paper, but we can pay a high performance price for these designs. A common problem in multi-tier designs is the remote communication overhead when large volumes of data have to be moved around, or in general when the resources to work with are on a different computer than the process doing the work.

Moving the worker-process to the computer with the resources is one solution. As mentioned in one of the introductory case studies, several relational databases (such as Oracle and DB2) now include a built-in JVM, so that we can deploy Java data processing applications directly inside of the database server (using JDBC).

A breaking point for this strategy is if moving new processes onto the target machine leads to excessive process switching, and the swapping overhead degrades performance. Using a built-in database JVM will avoid this potential problem.

1.6 ALGORITHM AND DATA STRUCTURE STRATEGIES

The previous performance suggestions do not require changing source code or the design of the software, and are thus a good place to start. However, improved hardware and JVMs can only take us so far, especially if the design is grossly inefficient. The intent of these strategies is to improve performance by changing the algorithms and data structures.

To start with, find out what is worth changing by profiling, in order to find the "hot spots" that are performance bottlenecks. Since 95% of execution time is usually spent in 5% of the code, it is very important to not waste time optimizing code that is seldom used. As previously discussed, a good profiler will provide a sorted report identifying what methods are executing the most, and what kind of objects are getting most frequently created.

It is worthwhile understanding how to estimate time and space complexity—a good reference is *Data Structures and Algorithm Analysis in Java* [Weiss 1998], which even discusses the Java 2 Collections API. In practice, it is worthwhile determining the complexity of the hot spot algorithms, so that informed insight can be applied to an improved design.

Not all the strategies we present include Java examples. For some, the implementation is straightforward or obvious (e.g., "cache *hashCode* results") or it is more easily understood by describing the algorithm, rather than showing pages of dense code.

Where we felt source code would help explain the technique, such as multiplexing socket connections, we have included listings.

CACHE REUSABLE THINGS

Saving or caching reusable things can have a profound impact on performance. It can avoid redoing expensive work, and reduce object creation and reclamation. Here are some examples of caching:

- **Cache windows.** When a user closes a window, rather than really close it, make it invisible. Store all invisible windows in a look-up table. When a user requests to open a window, retrieve it from the table and make it visible. A variation on this is that when the application starts up, a low level background thread works to create the most commonly used windows and stores their invisible versions in the look-up table. This variation is an example of *background future evaluation*. See Listing 1.1.

- **Cache bitmaps.** In a calendar and scheduling window suppose that the user can scroll from month-to-month and that on each month there are little iconic hints to indicate the presence of appointments. Rather than generate bitmaps on-the-fly, use a low-level background thread to generate the most common months and store them in a look-up table. As previously uncreated months are generated, store them in the table as well.

- **Cache hash codes.** If an object is being used as a hashed collection key, then a lookup operation will be faster if the hash code can be cached, rather than recalculated. Thus the *hashCode* method would return an instance field value. Naturally, if the hash code value becomes invalid due to object state change also used in the *equals* method, it is necessary to flush the cached value.

- **Cache *toString* results?** Caching the *toString* value may be worthwhile if the results are reused in the release version of the application, but if they are only used during debugging, it is a waste of space. If it is suitable to apply, then when *toString* is first called, initialize a string instance field with the appropriate string, and reuse that value on subsequent *toString* invocations. If the *toString* value becomes invalid due to object state change, it is necessary to flush the cached value.

- **Cache remote communication results.** Remote method communication over a network is *slow.* Therefore, it is desirable to cache the results of remote calls within the client. One common technique to achieve this is to define a single client-side *Facade* object [GHJV 1995] that funnels all potential remote calls. The client-side Facade caches the results of non-void remote calls, and avoids a remote call if it was previously made and has a cached result. Another approach is to make a client-side *Proxy* instance for each remote object, that caches remote call results. Whatever the variation, this technique is especially useful if the data is rarely updated, or the impact of slightly stale data is low—this is an example of *exploiting patterns in data.* Otherwise, the complication with this approach is the need for a synchronization protocol to update stale cached data.

- **Cache database query results and materialized objects.** In a middle-tier server, in response to client requests, a server can cache the results of JDBC queries in an in-memory lookup table, and serve up these cached results, rather than query the database again. Flexible refresh policies can be attached to the cacher so that, for example, a cached query result is discarded after one minute; within that interval, all client requests use the cached value. This is particularly useful for high-volume queries. Similarly, a middle-tier object server that "materializes" relational database values into objects can cache the materialized objects.

- **Cache mathematical values.** For example, if you know that particular ranges of trigonometry values are going to be used frequently, then store them in a table, because invocation of many *Math* trigonometry operations is expensive.

- **Cache loop invariants.** Calculate and save loop invariants in local variables, before a loop is entered. A good compiler will already do this for some cases.

- **Cache *String.getBytes* results.** Invoking *String.getBytes* is relatively slow; it is implicitly invoked within (slow) operations such as *writeUTF(String).* Therefore, for constant strings, it is better to cache the results (for example, in static byte arrays), and to use a *write(byte[])* operation instead.

- **Cache reflective element requests.** The reflective operations to retrieve elements, such as *Class.getMethod,* are relatively slow. Cache the results in a *Map* or field if they are needed again.

Example: Caching Windows

The following listings (Listing 1.1 and Listing 1.2) illustrate the use and implementation of a (very simple) object pool that uses background future evaluation to create anticipated slow-to-create windows and saves them in an object pool. The windows can be recycled, rather than re-created. Such object pools are a mechanism to both cache reusable things, and reduce object creation.

Listing 1.1 Create (slow to create) anticipated windows on a background thread in an object pool, and then display them later, when requested.

```
// simple factory that creates a window object

IObjectFactory factory = new IObjectFactory()
  {
    public Object createObject(){ return new TestJFrame(); }
  };

// create the pool

ObjectPool pool = new ObjectPool( factory );

// demonstrates creating a window on a background thread

pool.createObjectsAsync( 1, Thread.MIN_PRIORITY );

// ...
// later when a window is needed, get one previously created

JFrame frame = (JFrame) pool.getObject();
frame.setVisible( true );

// ...
// later, when the window is no longer needed, recycle it

frame.setVisible( false );
pool.replaceObject( frame );
```

The following object pool implementation shown in Listing 1.2 can have many variations and improvements. For example, one could specify a maximum size for the pool, and use lazy on-demand creation of objects rather than background creation.

Listing 1.2 A simple object pool implementation with background creation.

```java
import java.util.*;

/**
 * This class is responsible for creating objects
 * on a (usually low priority) thread, and then
 * providing them on request. It is assumed that
 * when the client is finished with the object,
 * it will be added back to the pool.
 */
public class ObjectPool
{
  private Stack resources = new Stack();
  private IObjectFactory factory;

  /**
   * Create an ObjectPool with the specified factory. The factory
   * is responsible for creating objects on demand.
   */
  public ObjectPool( IObjectFactory factory )
  {
    this.factory = factory;
  }

  public Object getObject()
  {
    synchronized( resources )
    {
      if ( !resources.isEmpty() )
        return resources.pop();
    }

    return factory.createObject();
  }

  public void replaceObject( Object object )
  {
    resources.push( object );
  }

  /**
   * Populate the pool with the specified number of objects on a
   * separate thread, at the specified priority.
   */
  public final void createObjectsAsync( final int number, int priority )
  {
    Thread thread = new Thread( new Runnable()
    {
      public void run() { createObjects( number ); }
    } );

    thread.setPriority( priority );
    thread.start();
  }
```

```
/**
 * Populate the pool with the specified number of objects.
 */
private void createObjects( int number )
{
  for ( int i = 0; i < number; i++ )
    resources.push( factory.createObject() );
}
}
```

```
public interface IObjectFactory
{
  Object createObject();
}
```

REDUCE OBJECT CREATION

Object creation in Java has these potentially negative performance implications:

- Object creation (allocation) is not blinding fast, so a program that creates *many* objects will probably have a performance hot spot with respect to creation.

- Overactive garbage collection may occur if there are many short-lived objects being created.

- A very large set of objects in memory may strain memory resources and lead to excessive paging.

Usually, it is not exactly the time of object creation that is the performance culprit, but rather the attendant problems that come from creating too many short-lived objects, such as overactive garbage collection. Note that this technique is most applicable when there are *many* short-lived objects being created.

Sometimes object creation is subtle, or seemingly innocuous code is creating more short-lived objects than we expected. For example, there is the well-known problem related to *String* concatenation, explored more fully in a later chapter. Consider the following snippet:

```
String s3 = s1 + s2 + s3;
```

This concatenation operation is actually achieved with a temporary (unseen) new *StringBuffer* object, which is discarded shortly after creation. In general, many operations may cause—behind the scenes—lots of short-lived object creation.

As another example, consider the method in Listing 1.3.

Listing 1.3 Using an Iterator.

```
public void foo()
{
   for ( Iterator i = myList.iterator(); i.hasNext(); )
   {
     Node node = (Node) i.next();
     // do some work with node
   }
}
```

Suppose that this *foo* method is called thousands of times from a loop in another method. The apparently innocuous *Iterator* object, used so often in collection manipulation algorithms, is a short-lived object being created and discarded thousands of times. We advocate the use of tolerators, but if this is a creation hot spot, we need to change the code into the following alternative, which avoids creating one.

Listing 1.4 Avoiding an Iterator.

```
public void foo()
{
   int max = myList.size();
   for ( int i = 0; i < max; i++ )
   {
     Node node = (Node) myList.get( i );
     // do some work with node
   }
}
```

Recycling Instances

One widely applicable technique to reduce object creation is to recycle instances rather than throw them away. For example, consider the method in Listing 1.5. Assume that a *Map* is keyed by *NodeKey* objects[1]. At ❶ a new instance of a *NodeKey* is created in order to search in a map; it is a very short-lived object. If this method is called frequently, this is an undesirable design.

Listing 1.5 This method creates unnecessary objects.

```
/**
 * Get an existing node, or create one.
 */
private Node getNodeFor( String key, Map map )
{
❶ NodeKey nodeKey = new NodeKey( key );
  Node n = (Node) map.get( nodeKey );

  if ( n == null )
  {
    n = new Node( key );
    map.put( new NodeKey( key ), n );
  }

  return n;
}
```

The solution is to save the short-lived object in an instance field, and reuse it, as shown in Listing 1.6.

Listing 1.6 Save a recyclable object in an instance field.

```
public final class DependencyGraph
{
➤ private NodeKey reusableKey = new NodeKey( "" );
  // ...

  /**
   * Get an existing node, or create one.
   */
  private Node getNodeFor( String key, Map map )
```

---

1. Why *NodeKey* rather than *String*? As explained in a later performance tip, indexing hash tables by *String* can be a performance problem.

```
{
     // avoid creating a new NodeKey instance each time

❶   reusableKey.setKey( key );
     Node n = (Node) map.get( reusableKey );

     if ( n == null )
     {
       n = new Node( key );
       map.put( new NodeKey( key ), n );
     }

     return n;
}
// ...
```

A word of caution on recycling instances: It can lead to designs that are not thread safe, unless synchronization is applied. For example, the revamped method in Listing 1.6 is no longer thread safe because two threads can enter the method and violate data safety on the *reusableKey*. If it is a multi-threaded application, the solution is to either synchronize this private method or synchronize all the public methods whose execution path can lead to this method.

In addition, the reused instance is being applied as a key in a map. Consequently, it is necessary that the *setKey* method invoked at ❶ updates the hash code of the *NodeKey* object. This hash code update should be very fast, to support the performance goals of this redesign.

Recycling Instances—Object (or Resource[1]) Pools

A common pattern to recycle instances is to create an **object pool**. This technique advises to pre-allocate a fixed number of recyclable instances and store them in a collection; perhaps creating them on a background thread. "New" instances are requested from the pool, and unneeded instances are returned to it.

Object pools are useful when many short-lived objects need to be continually created because it can reduce or eliminate overactive garbage collection. However, a

---

1. Although these are often generically called "resource" pools, note that the term "resource" is overloaded in Java to also especially mean external resources.

cautionary note: When a design requires the creation of a very large number of short-lived objects, it is better to first consider a redesign that eliminates the need altogether (e.g., use one recyclable instance), rather than applying a band-aid solution such as an object pool.

They are also useful for scarce resources or objects that take a relatively long time to create, such as threads or JDBC database connections. The technique described earlier of caching closed windows and then making them visible again when reopened can be considered a variation of the *Object Pool* pattern.

The object pool instance itself is often accessed via the *Singleton* pattern.

A word of caution on object pools used to improve creation speed and reduce garbage collection: As JVMs like HotSpot improve their allocation and garbage collection speeds, a naive implementation of an object pool may perform *worse* than what the JVM can natively provide. Be sure to do profiling, and verify that the object pool is helping, and not hindering performance.

Object (or resource) pools can create and manage their resources in several ways; typical variations include:

- A **bounded object pool**, which has an upper bound on objects, versus one that can grow unbounded. Object pools for scarce or "expensive" resources, such as threads, may be bounded pools.

- A lazy initialization scheme that creates and adds objects to the pool as they are requested, versus a pool that uses *background future evaluation* to create an anticipated set of (slow-to-create) objects on a low-priority background thread. Another alternative is an **eager initialization** scheme in which the objects are immediately created within the pool constructor—suitable if the objects are quickly instantiated.

A Thread Pool Example

For example, a **thread pool** may be a bounded pool that holds a collection of threads that are recycled to do work. It has the advantage of avoiding frequent *Thread* creation and reclamation, if many threads are used in a design, and it eliminates the delay of *Thread* creation, since the threads already exist. It can also be used to place an upper bound on the number of threads that will concurrently run, if thread thrashing or thread resources are a problem. Thread thrashing is discussed in the subsequent strategy to *use fewer threads*.

Note also that starting a thread in Java causes the allocation of an underlying native operating system thread, which can be a limited resource.[1] This motivates the need for thread pooling in a system such as a middle-tier application server, which will be called upon to create many threads.

To use the thread pool, create one with the total number of threads in the pool. Then send it a *run* message with a *Runnable* object. The *run* method will block until a thread is available to service the *Runnable*. See Listing 1.7.

Listing 1.7 Using a ThreadPool.

```
ThreadPool pool = new ThreadPool( 2 );

pool.run( new Runnable()
   {
      public void run()
      {
         for ( int i = 0; i < loopCount; i++ )
            System.out.println( "runner 1 " + i );
      }
   } );

pool.run( new Runnable()
   {
      // do some other work ...
   } );
```

The following thread pool implementation is a bounded pool that uses eager initialization (of course, lazy initialization or background future evaluation are alternatives). In the common case, clients will quickly obtain a thread, unless all threads are busy, in which case the requestor will block until a thread is free.

The *ThreadPool* maintains a queue of *Runnable* objects. A call to *Queue.get* will block until there is something to remove from the queue; a call to *Queue.put* adds to the queue and notifies the blocked threads waiting for data (see Listing 1.8).

---

1. An exception is that JVMs running on operating systems without native threads will only use JVM-internal "simulated" threads.

Listing 1.8 The Queue class.

```
public class Queue implements java.io.Serializable
{
  private List list = new ArrayList();

  /**
   *  Add obj to the queue and notify threads waiting in get() for data
   */
  synchronized public void put( Object obj )
  {
    list.add( obj );
    notify();
  }

  /**
   *  Suspend threads in a wait until there is data, then pop it.
   */
  synchronized public Object get()
  {
    while( list.isEmpty() )
      try { wait(); } catch( InterruptedException ex ) {}

    return list.remove( 0 );
  }
}
```

As illustrated in Listing 1.9, a *ThreadPool* object creates a set of *ThreadPoolThreads*, each of which starts running and waits on the *ThreadPool* queue for the next *Runnable* object that needs running.

Listing 1.9 The ThreadPool class.

```
public class ThreadPool
{
  private Queue runnableTasks = new Queue();

  public ThreadPool( int threadCount )
  {
    for ( int i = 0; i < threadCount; i++ )
    {
        ThreadPoolThread thread = new ThreadPoolThread( this );
        thread.start();
    }
  }

  /**
   * Add a task to the queue. A free thread will execute it.
   */
  public void run( Runnable task )
  {
```

```
        runnableTasks.put( task );
    }

    public Runnable getNextRunnable()
    {
        return (Runnable) runnableTasks.get();
    }
}
```

The *ThreadPoolThread* objects obtain a reference to their *ThreadPool*, and start running in an infinite loop. They wait to extract the next *Runnable* object from the *ThreadPool* queue, and then execute it (see Listing 1.10).

Listing 1.10 The ThreadPoolThread class.

```
public class ThreadPoolThread extends Thread
{
    private ThreadPool pool;

    public ThreadPoolThread( ThreadPool pool )
    {
        this.pool = pool;
    }

    /**
     * Run in an infinite loop, getting tasks to perform, or
     * blocking until work is available.
     */
    public void run()
    {
        while( true )
        {
            // this operation will block until a task is present

            Runnable task = pool.getNextRunnable();
            try { task.run(); } catch ( Exception ex ) {}
        }
    }
}
```

The previous sample implementation represents the basic idea of a thread pool; it could be enhanced to define threads of different priorities, among other refinements.

Shareable

Another very common technique to reduce object creation is the *Shareable* pattern [ABW 1997] which is used to share instances rather than duplicate them. It is very similar to the *Flyweight* pattern [GHJV 1995], which is slightly more constrained, and may be considered a special case of *Shareable*.

For example, suppose that there are thousands of *Address* objects with associated *USState* objects. There are only 50 American states, so it is undesirable to duplicate these thousands of times; it consumes both excessive time and space. The *Shareable* pattern suggests the following: During initialization create a collection that is initialized with these 50 instances, and indeed any other instances that are to be shared. When an *Address* object needs to be associated with a *USState* object, it is retrieved from a share pool, which is usually nothing more than a glorified lookup table. The share pool instance itself is generally accessed via the *Singleton* pattern. A variation is to maintain different share pools for different categories of objects. In summary, the *Shareable* pattern is very straightforward—simply storing shareable objects in a table.

An implication of the *Shareable* pattern is that a shared instance needs to be either immutable (read-only), stateless, or it is true that a change to a shared object can correctly apply to all objects that share it.

Notice in the following example that the shareable objects need to be indexed by a key, which in this case was probably obtained from a GUI widget for choosing the American state.

```
USState state = (USState) SharePool.getInstance().getObjectFor( key );
address.setState( state );
```

DO MORE IN EACH STEP, WHEN THE OVERHEAD OF EACH STEP IS HIGH

Several of the case studies illustrated this principle. Here are some examples:

- **Batch remote work**. Remote method invocation is relatively expensive; using fine-grained remote methods that mirror a design appropriate for local methods will noticeably reduce performance. Two common approaches are:

  - ❑ (most common) Make larger-grained remote operations that do more work. If these methods return information, design them to return an aggregate of results.

  - ❑ Another variation is to send a collection of operation requests (*Command* objects) as a parameter in one remote method invocation, process the commands (tasks) sequentially or in parallel on the server side, and return an aggregate result.

- **Batch operations within one database transaction**. In some databases, the start and commit operations of a transaction are relatively slow. A solution is to represent database operations (create, update, and delete) as *DatabaseCommand* objects and queue them. A large set of these can be processed within one transaction. An implication of this, however, is a loss of the "isolated" aspect of the ACID[1] nature of individual transactions, since several logical transactions are being grouped in one physical transaction. Recovery will be very difficult in the event of database operation failure, so this approach should only be considered if failure is very unlikely, or the cost of failure is negligible.

- **Look for and use existing "batch" operations in your libraries** (JDK or third party). For example, in some JVMs and JDK implementations, *Graphics.drawPolygon* is much faster than repeated calls to *Graphics.drawLine*.

- **Download a collection of elements in a JAR file**. Because of the overhead associated with each network file transfer, download performance is improved by grouping classes and resource files (such as images) in a JAR file.

---

1. ACID—atomic, consistent, isolated, durable. Four properties of reliable database transactions.

USE LARGE-GRAINED REMOTE COMMUNICATION

This is a reiteration and specialization of *do more in each step, when the overhead of each step is high*. However, it is worth stressing as a separate strategy, since it is such a common problem in distributed systems (for which Java is a popular choice).

One of the case studies at the beginning of this chapter described an application which monitored remote devices; it represented a common scenario where remote communication was a performance problem.

With the increasing popularity of Enterprise JavaBean (EJB) servers and the use of EntityBeans (which represent persistent objects in a database) this strategy will take on increased significance. When using EJB and EntityBeans, it makes for a simple (but ultimately doomed) design to perform a query to obtain remote references to possibly hundreds or thousands of EntityBean objects, which are then displayed in a *JTable*, one per row. The defect is that filling the table will result in thousands of remote method invocations, so the remote communication overhead of this very fine-grained remote object communication will kill application performance.

Instead, to get suitable performance with EJB (or similar contexts) when wishing to display a table view of many *EntityBean* objects, we can use the *Serialized Light-Weight Object Collection* strategy described next.

A potential breaking point with this technique relates to the observation that it often trades off lots of fine-grained remote invocations for fewer invocations that pass more serialized data. Distributed transmission of lots of serialized data again decreases the performance of remote method invocation.

USE SERIALIZED LIGHTWEIGHT OBJECT COLLECTIONS[1] FOR VIEWING AND UPDATING LARGE REMOTE DATASETS

Many applications need to present a GUI table view on a large dataset (such as a table in a relational database), and provide update capabilities on the row values. In the context of EJB, this could be done with many *EntityBean* instances, one per row. But as discussed in the previous section this is not feasible because the massive fine-grained remote method invocation will significantly harm performance.

The essence of the solution is to return a serialized collection (return by-value) of serialized lightweight objects representing a dataset that contains a *minimal* set of attributes required for browsing. Each object also includes a unique key by which the real, complete remote object can be found. It is important that the lightweight objects be as small as possible, to reduce the performance impact of transmitting lots of serialized data. When a user wants to see the complete version of an object, they make a GUI gesture on the lightweight version (such as double-clicking) that then causes the complete version to be retrieved and displayed. Figure 1.6 illustrates the remote communication.

Figure 1.6 Serialized lightweight object collections.

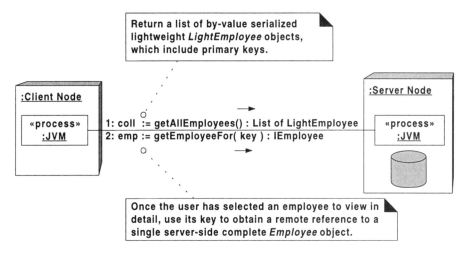

---

1. We know, it's a mouthful... These lightweight objects have also been called *skeleton* objects, but in the context of remote communication, this can be confused with the terminology of remote proxy skeleton objects in RMI and CORBA, which are different.

In more detail, the solution is:

1. Identify a *small* subset of attributes to be displayed in the *JTable*. For example, three columns of important data instead of an original ten. An essential attribute that must be included is a unique or primary key by which the real object (e.g., an EntityBean) can be found, although of course the key need not be displayed.

2. Design a remote Facade-like object (such as an EJB SessionBean) to return a serialized by-value collection of these lightweight abridged data objects.

3. Design the GUI in a "summary-detail" style in which a read-only *JTable* displays the summary information in the top portion of the window. For a selected row (object), an input gesture will cause a display of its complete information in a detail section at the bottom of the window.

4. The read-only *JTable* displays the (local) abridged data objects.

5. When the user wishes to update a row (e.g., an EntityBean instance), s/he performs some gesture, such as double clicking on the row.

6. The unique key for the selected abridged object is used to get a remote reference to the complete (remote) object. For example, the key could be used with an EJB *Home* object to obtain a reference to a remote EntityBean instance.

7. All the attributes of the complete remote object are displayed in the detail view section of the window. Update operations may also be supported.

EXPLOIT PATTERNS IN THE DATA

The introductory case study involving a help generator demonstrates that patterns may exist in the data that can be used to help optimize an application.

As another example, computer simulation of physical processes (e.g., weather modeling, oil flow modeling) is done using a technique called the **finite difference method**. Running the simulation involves constructing many very large arrays representing constraints in linear equations. It turns out that these arrays are very **sparse**—meaning that most cells are not used, or contain zeros. This sparse pattern in the data can be exploited to make a memory efficient **sparse matrix** data structure, in which only the cells actually used are allocated.

Another simple example of this strategy is the use of *RunArrays*. In many cases involving large sets of characters or numbers, it is known that there will often be repeating sequences of the same value—often for dozens or hundreds of times. This is known as a **run**, which has a run length that defines the number of repetitions. This is common with audio, video, and natural phenomena observations, and these run patterns are exploited by compression algorithms. If space is more important than speed, then a *RunArray* data structure can be defined that only stores the run value once, plus a run length count. Public methods to access individual elements of the array derive and return a particular element by calculation against the internal run structures.

EXPLOIT PATTERNS IN USAGE

For example:

- Data that is used together should be saved physically close together ("optimal locality of reference"), to maximize database cache utilization (which will improve I/O performance). If data is physically close, it is likely to be on the same database page, which is the typical unit of database caching granularity.

  - As an example of how to achieve this, some object databases give you control over where new objects will be physically stored. It is difficult to predict the optimal physical clustering of data at design time, which is very context sensitive. *Policy* or *Strategy* objects can be used that encapsulate a clustering policy. An administrator GUI can adjust these policies, based on an analysis of data usage patterns.

- Distribute Java middle-tier server processes to improve service and throughput, based on patterns in usage.

  - For example, distribute processes to maximize database cache utilization based on usage patterns. Suppose that there is only *one* middle-tier server, responding to requests A and B from different clients. Also suppose that the database data required for requests A and B is disjoint. Finally, assume that the data for either request A or B essentially fills the database cache. Then, interleaving requests to perform A, then B, then A, then B, ... will cause the cache to be reloaded for each operation. Thus, the cache is thrashing and we are not receiving any benefit from it. If the cache size is at its maximum, then a solution is to create *two* servers, one that serves request A, and another which serves request B. Now, each will make optimal use of its database cache. More generally, this is an example of *partitioning bottleneck resources*.

  ☐ As another example, consider a "stock quote and trader" server. There is a very high request rate for stock quotes, but relatively few trade requests. The high quote request load may reduce the service level for trade requests, because the quote requests cause frequent consumption of thread, socket, and database connection resources. That is, traders may have to wait longer than desired to complete a trade operation, because they are swamped by the quote requestors. By moving the trade operations onto a separate trader-server, throughput can be improved. This is an example of load-balancing based upon the frequency of operation types, which is a specialization of exploiting patterns in usage.

■ In general, optimize databases and SQL as hinted at in the *effectively use SQL* suggestion later in this section.

EXPLOIT IDLE PROCESSOR TIME WITH BACKGROUND FUTURE EVALUATION

This strategy is a variation of *exploit patterns in data and usage* and of *caching*. In some situations it is possible to anticipate likely results or objects that will be needed in the near future. For example:

■ Certain windows will probably be opened.

■ Predictable data will likely soon be requested from a database or server, based on current data that has been retrieved, entered, or requested.

  ☐ Suppose that on a *StudentSummaryWindow* there are a few data fields to enter, the first being a student's ID. And further suppose that it is often the case that the user will soon request a secondary *StudentHistoryWindow* showing all past student courses and grades. If this is so, then once the student ID is entered on the first window, a background thread can get busy fetching the history data, in anticipation of likely use.

   ❑ If a **lazy collection** (described later) is being used to fault in ranges of data for display in a *JTable* view, then the next range to fault in (that is below the current range being scrolled through by the user) can be loaded while the user is looking at currently loaded data.

■ Predictable work will be requested in the near future. For example, in a word processor spell checking can be performed on a background thread while the user is typing.

If there is some idle processor time, such as when a user is simply looking at a window, or when a middle-tier server is not handling requests, then use that time to evaluate probable future requests on low priority background threads, and cache the results.

Extending the likely-windows example, at application start up, initiate a low priority background thread that creates the most likely windows, but does not make them visible. Once created, cache them. When the window must be displayed, retrieve it from the cache, via a *WindowFactory*, for example.

We recommend that results and expensive new objects be requested from a *Factory* object [GHJV 1995], which can either return a cached, pre-evaluated object that was created on a background future evaluation thread, or which can generate the results on-demand, using lazy initialization. Using the Factory object decouples the clients from whichever strategy is taken. For example:

```
// Factory may return cached results generated by background
// thread, or create the requested results.

JFrame win1 = (JFrame) WindowFactory.getInstance().
                    getNewWindow( WindowFactory.WIN_TYPE1 );
```

The tricky part of this strategy is the synchronization between the Factory and background thread with the future evaluation work plan.

Since many threads can lead to performance degradation simply because of the overhead of thread management and context switching, we recommend only one or two background future evaluation threads. A *BackgroundFutureInitializer* object, on its own low-priority thread, can follow a prioritized agenda of anticipatory work (a work plan) to accomplish. The work can be represented as various *Command* objects in a priority queue [GHJV 1995], with polymorphic *execute* methods that perform different tasks, such as creating windows, pre-fetching data, and so on.

A breaking point of this technique comes when new objects are requested in rapid succession or object creation takes a very long time relative to the amount of idle time. In these cases, the overhead and lock contention can reduce overall performance.

A minor variation on this design is to use many fine-grained **Future Evaluator** objects or **futures** [HM 1998]. For each future result a new Future Evaluator active object is created and started—each with its own low priority thread of execution. The design is clean and simple, but a disadvantage is possible thread explosion, and subsequent performance degradation.

INCREASE PROCESS PARALLELISM

Some problems can, to some degree, be split into parallel tasks running in different processes. For example, simulation problems representing physical space may be geometrically decomposed into large sub-blocks of physical space, which are distributed for simulation onto multiple processors. Sometimes synchronization is required at regular intervals between the divided parts of the problem; the designer must be careful that the overhead of this synchronization does not wipe out the gains made by the division of labor.

USE NATIVE METHODS

For the many Java applications for which there is no need for cross-platform portability, native methods that invoke functions written in C or C++ can provide significant performance improvements.

A breaking point with native methods is to note that the "travel" cost from Java to a native method and back is relatively slow. Thus, even if the native method is fast, the overhead may negate the potential improvement. As is usual when the overhead of each step is high, the solution is to do more work in each step: Implement native methods that do more work, or that do a "batch" of work, rather than just a small task.

USE MORE THREADS

One motivation for using multiple threads is to *exploit idle processor time* to do other required work, or to execute anticipated work in the background, in order to improve overall throughput or performance. Processors may be idle due to a thread waiting on a resource (usually blocking I/O such as slow input from a database, or a slow file load over the Internet), waiting for a request to do work (such as in a server), or because a person is looking at a user interface rather than interacting with a computer. Note also that the growing popularity of symmetric multiprocessor architectures increases the amount of idle processor time on compute nodes.[1]

The strategy to *exploit idle processor time with background future evaluation* is an example of how using more threads can improve throughput.

USE FEWER THREADS

The Dark Side of Threads is their ability to cause a degradation of throughput or performance. In addition to potential problems with deadlock and starvation, there is the overhead of thread management and context switching. At some point, too many threads will cause a state of **thrashing**, in which throughput dramatically drops because of excessive time spent in thread overhead. The number of threads at which thrashing occurs varies widely—it is dependent on the amount of work in

---

1. Probably the most ambitious project to exploit idle processor time is the Search for Extraterrestrial Intelligence (SETI) "screen saver" program SETI@Home (available at www.seti.org). The screen saver downloads chunks of unanalyzed radio telescope data and analyzes it, returning the results to SETI on completion. Hundreds of thousands of people are participating.

each thread, their priority, and the native threading support provided by the operating system, among other factors.[1]

One technique to reduce thread usage is to use a bounded thread pool (with a maximum number of threads), as discussed earlier. Such a thread pool will block requests for work until a thread is free to do work. A caveat with this approach is that deadlock is possible, although rare in practice.

Another technique to reduce the number of threads—to decrease the possibility of thrashing—while still maintaining some concurrency for background tasks is to create a *TaskProcessor* active object which runs on its own single thread. The *TaskProcessor* maintains a priority queue (e.g., a *SortedSet* implementation) of *Command* objects which represent arbitrary tasks to perform (all with polymorphic *execute* methods). Each command may have its own priority value, which defines its order in the priority queue. The *TaskProcessor* executes each command object, in turn. This design is an alternative to creating a separate thread for each background task.

EFFECTIVELY USE SQL AND A FAST JDBC DRIVER

Here are some pointers and qualities to consider when using databases and JDBC.

- First, the most important performance tip is to design a high performance database, and use SQL skillfully. In general, these strategies are usually specializations of *exploiting patterns in data and usage*. Appropriate database indexing, database tuning, choice of disk technology, and so-called "tricky" SQL can make enormous performance gains. These topics are outside of our scope, but there are many excellent online and text resources available. In addition to the "SQL tips" material from your database vendor (which is a good place to start), an excellent adjunct is the text *Joe Celko's SQL for Smarties: Advanced SQL Programming* [Celko 1999].

---

1. Third-party Java tools are available which visualize thread activity, and will highlight a suspected thrashing condition, indicated by frequent change of state of the threads, with little or no apparent time spent in any thread.

■ Use *CallableStatements* (stored procedures) and database triggers (database-side event-driven procedures) for the fastest processing; do the work in the database. This is a variation of *do more in each step, when the overhead of each step is high.* With the advent of JVM's integrated into relational databases, and the use of Java as a stored procedure language, the server-side can also be written in Java. This eliminates a prior disadvantage of stored procedures: that they were written in proprietary, non-portable languages.

■ Use *PreparedStatements* instead of regular *Statements*—static compiled SQL is much faster than dynamic SQL if the statement is invoked more than once (there is overhead fetching the *PreparedStatement* on its first invocation). Note that *PreparedStatements* can be flexibly parameterized with binding variables (or IN parameters, in JDBC terms) using a "?" as a placeholder. For example, SELECT * FROM EMP WHERE ID = ?.

■ A *Statement* (or *ResultSet)* should be given two hints in order to improve performance. *Statement.setFetchSize* hints at how many rows to fetch at a time from the database. If you know that many rows will be processed, set this to a large value. *Statement.setFetchDirection* hints at the direction in which the rows will be processed (forward, reverse, or random).

■ Use updateable *ResultSets,* and update them programmatically in Java, rather than using SQL UPDATE and INSERT operations. An updateable version is created by passing *ResultSet.CONCUR_UPDATABLE* to one of the *Statement* creation methods (such as *Connection.prepareStatement*). The *ResultSet.update<Type>* methods update cells, *ResultSet.moveToInsertRow* adds a new row, and the *ResultSet.updateRow* method applies the updates to the database.

■ Use the JDBC batch commands *Statement.addBatch* and *Statement.executeBatch* for faster batch SQL processing of INSERT, UPDATE, and DELETE operations.

■ Turn *autocommit* off.

Here are some qualities to consider in choosing a high-performance JDBC driver:

■ JDBC 2.0 compliant driver.

- If a type 2 native API version is available, use it if possible (because it will probably be the fastest type of driver).

- Database connection pooling.

- Caching of prior fetches.

- Proactive fetching of rows likely to be requested.

- Parallel support—can be used in multi-threaded applications without serializing all requests.

REDUCE HIGH FREQUENCY DYNAMIC BINDING

This is a variation of *do more in each step, when the overhead of each step is high* and *promote inlined methods*. However, it is worth stressing as a separate strategy, since it is a common problem in object design.

In Java, the overhead of dynamically binding to the appropriate virtual method is very small. However, in some performance critical contexts, such as intensive engineering and scientific computing with *billions* of method invocations, the overhead can be devastating, especially because virtual methods can not be inlined. To reiterate, dynamic binding contexts prevent the compiler from inlining, which is a significant loss of an important optimization.

Consequently, it is sometimes desirable to replace dynamic binding calls to virtual methods with calls to non-virtual methods, to reduce this small overhead and most especially to allow the compiler to increase inlining.

"Classic" object-oriented designs in which behavior and data are placed together (or close together) tend to encourage high frequency *fine-grained* use of polymorphism and dynamic binding. Although elegant and easy to adapt, and a sensible first choice when designing systems, these designs may not cut it performance-wise. We may be forced to "de-objectize" the design, if you will.

A common design idiom to replace fine-grained polymorphism is to remove polymorphic methods from the offending fine-grained objects and redesign them as "passive" data objects. Then the objects are placed in sets that represent what kind of operation to perform on them; for example, a *CalculationSet*. The *Strategy* pattern (representing an algorithm as an object) is used to flexibly attach varying algorithms to the *CalculationSet* objects. The Strategy objects are applied to each passive data object in the set. The dynamic binding has been pushed up to a higher, more coarse-grained level—at the set level rather than at the individual instance level.

This design style of applying Strategy algorithms to sets of objects (to achieve lower-frequency coarser-grained dynamic binding) is a variation of what has been called **generic programming**. It is widely used in C++ in the Standard Template Library (STL) design, and in the design of the Java Generic Library (JGL).

An Example

For example, simulation is a common technique in engineering and scientific computing applications such as simulating the flow of water, oil, and gas underground, as wells extract oil.

A common simulation technique involves organizing a physical space (such as an oil reservoir) into a three-dimensional grid of *millions* of cells (for example, 10x10x10 meter underground blocks), associating properties with each cell (such as oil pressure and saturation), and running a simulation over many time steps such that each cell influences its neighbor's properties.

In the case of oil reservoir simulation, a cell can change "state" by containing mostly oil or mostly water. The algorithm for calculating the cell density changes when the cell changes state. A classic object-oriented design would use the State pattern [GHJV 1995] to provide varying density algorithms, as the cell state changes (Figure 1.7). Although an elegant design, it is inefficient because *billions* of dynamic binding calls will be made during a simulation run, with no chance for the compiler to optimize using inlined methods.

An altenative design (Figure 1.8) places passive data cells into container objects called *CalculationSets*. Cells in the oil state are placed in one *CalculationSet* instance for oil cells, water state cells go in another set. Strategy objects, such as Strategies to calculate cell density, are attached to a *CalculationSet* instance, to allow for flexible attachment or replacement of algorithms. When a cell changes state, it is moved to a different set. It is known that reservoir cells change state slowly, so the shuffling overhead does not negate the performance gains of this design (an example of *exploit patterns in the data*).

Figure 1.7 A "classic" object-oriented design with excessive dynamic binding.

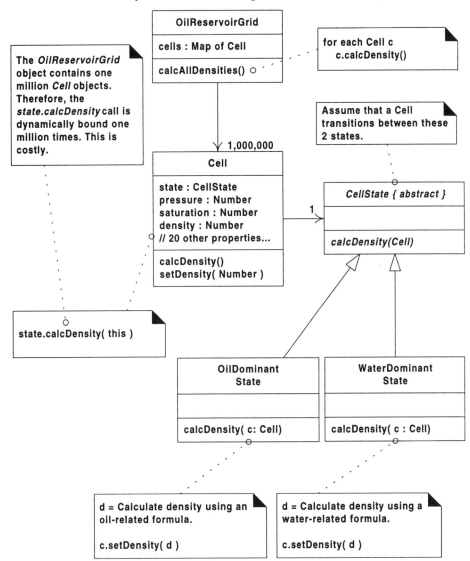

Figure 1.8 Applying the Strategy pattern to reduce dynamic binding.

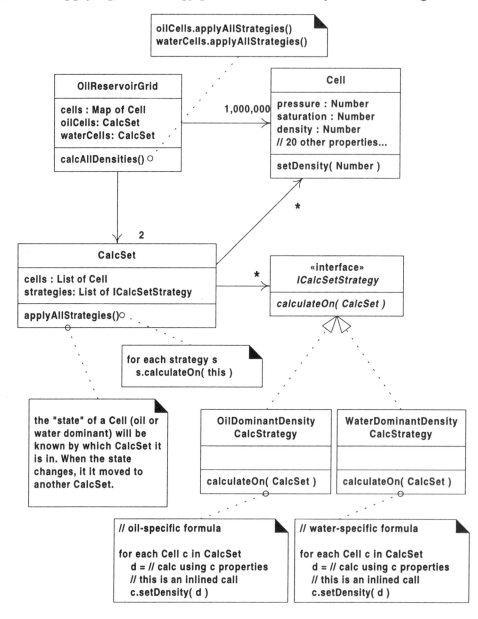

USE A HIGH-PERFORMANCE EJB APPLICATION SERVER

If you are developing a distributed middle-tier application in Java, you should seriously consider using an Enterprise JavaBeans (EJB) application server to improve performance—in addition to using EJB for its value in simplifying development. EJB server vendors are aggressively competing on performance and scalability (among other features). For example, EJB servers include resource (or object) pooling of threads and database connections, and possibly pooling of reusable Session-Bean instances. Similar to the evolution of optimized database products, EJB servers will become increasingly fine-tuned by the vendors to optimize their remote communication handling, JNDI implementations, distributed transaction support, JDBC drivers, and so on.

FOR CONNECTION SCALABILITY, USE SERVER PRODUCTS WITH MULTIPLEXING SOCKET CONNECTIONS OR UDP MESSAGING

Multiplexing Socket Connections

In a client-server application, a client will typically initiate a network conversation to a server. If the conversation is held over TCP/IP, the client will have to open a socket to the server. This socket is used to read and write bytes to and from the server. If the client is multithreaded, each thread of control carries on a separate conversation with the server. The naive implementation of this multithreaded client-server conversation allocates a separate socket for each thread—that is, a separate socket for each conversation.

This is usually fine for the client, which typically has on the order of tens of threads, and thus only needs tens of sockets. For the server, however, this kind of socket allocation policy can be disastrous. A server serving hundreds of clients can easily require over a thousand sockets. Unfortunately, sockets are among the most precious of resources and many operating systems have difficulty scaling to this kind of load.

The solution is to implement a multiplexing socket connection. A multiplexing socket connection allows a client and a server to establish many virtual client-to-server socket connections using only one real socket at each end. When using multiplexing socket connections, all threads on the client-side will share a single "client-side multiplexing connection" object. All client-side threads will communicate via this shared connection object to write to a server, rather than opening multiple socket connections. This means that the number of server-side sockets is precisely equal to the number of clients connected to the server.

Implementing a multiplexing socket requires that both the client and server side share a contract to use a common multiplexing protocol. The heart of the solution is that every message to a server, and reply message from a server, should contain a message ID. A reply message from the server to the client will contain the same ID as the original initiating message from the client. In this way, the client can match up reply messages with sent messages, and with threads waiting for a reply. In addition, the client-side multiplexing connection object must contain some slightly fancy synchronization and wait-notify logic.

It is less common that an application developer will need to directly implement a multiplexing socket. Rather, it is most often used within the plumbing of an ORB-like product such as an RMI implementation, CORBA ORB, ObjectSpace Voyager, EJB servers, "application server," and so on. If you are planning to build a Java server application that must scale up for many connections, check that your underlying ORB-like technology uses multiplexing sockets. If you have to grow your own scalable server using low-level techniques instead of an application server, consider implementing multiplexing sockets.

UDP Messaging

The *DatagramSocket* class provides an unreliable, connectionless datagram connection between a client and server—that is, it provides a UDP connection. Because one *DatagramSocket* can send to many hosts (and ports), and also act as a receiver from many clients, UDP can more easily scale up than TCP with respect to the number of concurrent connections. In addition, the absence of the connection-oriented reliable delivery that TCP provides makes UDP a faster protocol. In applications where guaranteed delivery of a packet is not critical, such as streaming audio, UDP is a better choice than TCP.

The price paid for better performance in UDP is unreliable delivery. However, there are protocols that can be used with it in order to provide—in some cases—faster reliable delivery than TCP (in contradiction to the original intent of UDP); so-called **reliable UDP**. The most common are variations of a **sliding-window protocol**, which is also used in TCP. In certain application and network contexts, with context-sensitive tuned values for the "window size," reliable UDP can outperform TCP. However, a potential danger in implementing this approach is to essentially re-invent TCP, and not gain anything. Since the reliability layer of TCP is probably efficiently implemented in C or even assembler, it may be hard to beat.

1.7 THE HOTSPOT JVM: AN OVERVIEW

This section provides an introduction to the technology behind HotSpot, for those curious about its implementation.

Adaptive Compilation in HotSpot

HotSpot works best on applications that repeatedly run the same sections of code, and that run for "a while," because its key performance enhancement is the use of **adaptive compilation**. HotSpot launches an application using a standard bytecode interpreter. It profiles the application while it runs and identifies bottlenecks in performance—hot spots. It then adaptively performs an *informed* optimizing native-code compilation on the hot spots, using techniques such as **inlining** (replacing a call to a method with the body of the method being called). The resulting native machine code for the hot spots is cached in memory. Subsequent invocation of a hotspot method uses the cached (and optimized) machine code, rather than byte-code interpretation. Execution of machine code is of course much faster than byte-code interpretation. Furthermore, this is high-quality *optimized* machine code, because HotSpot has profiling information with which to make context-specific, informed, optimal compilation decisions.

As a corollary of this behavior, if an application does not repeatedly invoke the adaptively compiled code, no significant performance improvements will be seen with HotSpot. This situation will arise if the application shuts down shortly after adaptive compilation was applied (or before it ever is), or (rarely) because of some capricious change in behavior that regularly moves the application on to new sections of code shortly after adaptive compilation in the prior section, which is no longer executed.

A technique that JIT compilers use to obtain further (minor) performance enhancements is to generate native code that does *not* pre-check for null pointers, or array out of bounds exceptions. However, HotSpot v1.0 still generates native code with bounds checking, but it is on the HotSpot development team's to-do list to remove this checking in a future version, to further enhance performance.

Fast Garbage Collection in HotSpot

HotSpot includes an improved garbage collector that is "faster and more efficient than the garbage collector in the Java 2 SDK." A key technique is the use of a **generational collector** that organizes objects into different areas, according to their age or generation. It exploits the fact that on average about 95% of objects are very short-lived. New objects are created contiguously in an object "nursery"—a large block of memory. A new object is quickly allocated in stack-like manner at the beginning of the unused portion of the block; the block fills up from beginning to end. A "free" pointer is updated to always point to the beginning of the remaining unused portion, and can be quickly tested to see if the fixed-sized block is about to overflow (the next object to add is larger than the remaining space).

When nursery overflow is about to occur, the collector enters a clean-up phase. It identifies all objects in the nursery that are still "alive" (have active references to them). On average, this is only about 5% of the objects. It copies these live objects to a separate "Old Object" memory area (OOMA). It then sets the "free" pointer back to the beginning of the nursery block, and starts contiguously filling it again, as new objects are created. Note that no reclamation work (searching for and compacting garbage-collected memory) was required for the many short-lived dead objects; the same nursery block is simply reused from the start.

To avoid overflow in the OOMA, HotSpot provides two alternative collection schemes:

1. This first scheme—which is the default for HotSpot—is a **mark-compact** collector[1] that *only* runs if the OOMA is low on free space. It is the default because the alternative pauseless scheme causes a decrease in overall performance. In mark-compact mode, when memory is low, the collector traverses the graphs of all objects rooted at live objects. Any object in the OOMA that is not in the graphs is dead. In other words, dead objects in the OOMA can be identified. The remaining live objects are compacted together, thus opening up a contiguous free block at the end of the OOMA that newly entering "old agers" from the nursery can use. Unfortunately, the defect with this scheme is potentially "long" pauses when the collector is initiated, the length of the pause being proportional to the number of live objects. However, unless an application is very time sensitive this pause is still so short that it is not a concern.

2. The second scheme is an incremental, *pauseless* Old Object collector. In this mode, a background daemon thread is always performing old object garbage collection, but in very regular, short steps (on the order of a few milliseconds at regular intervals). In contrast to the default mark-compact scheme, which can cause a longer pause, this scheme smooths out the work in continuous, regular small steps. However, the defect with the pauseless approach is an overall decrease in performance. Sun estimates an average 10% performance decrease in version 1.0 of HotSpot, but for our benchmark application the decrease was greater—it caused HotSpot to run at about the same speed as in the old JIT JVM (see Figure 1.3). This is sure to improve in future versions. A pauseless collector is advantageous in time-sensitive applications, such as real-time systems. To turn on the incremental garbage collector in HotSpot, use the -*Xincgc* option:

---

1. Also known as a mark-and-sweep collector.

```
>java -Xincgc foo.Main
```

Fast Thread Synchronization in HotSpot

HotSpot includes an optimization so that the overhead of thread synchronization is negligible. With early JVMs there was a significant performance penalty in calling methods that included the *synchronized* modifier. HotSpot essentially eliminates this overhead.

To measure the synchronization overhead in HotSpot, we wrote a testing program that called identical methods, except that one was synchronized. In 1,000,000 invocations, synchronization added only 800 milliseconds of overhead—roughly 0.00001 milliseconds of overhead per invocation. In short, negligible.

Of course, by definition a synchronized method reduces concurrency by providing only serialized access to a method, one thread at a time; reducing concurrency can still have a very significant design-level impact on performance. HotSpot simply eliminates the overhead of lock management on synchronized methods. In a multi-threaded application, synchronized designs are inherently slower than unsynchronized designs, regardless of lock management overhead.

Another indirect way that synchronized methods can slow performance is by preventing inlining during compile-time optimization. Synchronized methods can not be inlined, and thus prevent a JIT compiler or HotSpot from applying this useful optimization.

HotSpot versus JIT Compiler JVMs

A JIT JVM works by translating the bytecode for a method into machine code, the first time the method is invoked, and caching the machine code in memory. Subsequent invocation of the method just executes the cached machine code. A JIT JVM does this for every invoked method.

A JIT JVM has several native code generation hurdles to overcome, that HotSpot may have an advantage with. These include:

- For a JIT compiler, excellent optimized machine code is harder to generate since it must work quickly (to avoid long user-time pauses) and does not have contextual profiling information, because it must compile the bytecode before the method has executed. In contrast, HotSpot can compile slowly and carefully, on a background thread, and use profiling results from the bytecode interpreter to produce ideal machine code for the critical sections of code.

- JIT compilers translate *all* the bytecode of invoked methods into machine code. This cached machine code consumes a fair amount of memory. In contrast, HotSpot creates and caches less machine code—only for the hot spots of code that are frequently executed.

- Inlining is an important optimization strategy that both JITs and HotSpot apply. Due to profiling information, HotSpot has the capacity to inline the most appropriate methods in order to maximize the value of inlining. A JIT must make inlining decisions without knowledge of what is most valuable to inline.

Time will tell if these hurdles always give HotSpot (or similar adaptive compiler JVMs) an ongoing advantage over JIT compilers. It may be the case that a combination of very high speed JIT native compilation, faster processors, and a growing body of refined JIT compiler heuristics lead to JIT compilers that outperform HotSpot.

The Java Plug-In and HotSpot

The Java Plug-In technology that is included in the Java 2 SDK is used to replace the default JVM used in a browser with another JVM and library, such as HotSpot. Note that a bug in SDK v1.2.1 prevented that version from being used with HotSpot as the plug-in.

2 IMPROVING PERFORMANCE— MODERATE-MINOR

In this chapter

- Optimization techniques which are likely to make a moderate or only minor improvement.

PROMOTE INLINED METHODS

An inlined method replaces a call to a method with the body of the method. This can produce a meaningful optimization when the method is frequently invoked, because it eliminates the relatively expensive overhead of the method invocation, which also involves the expense of reallocating registers for the called method. If we use the HotSpot JVM with its adaptive optimizing compiler, use an optimizing JIT JVM, or compile with an "optimize" option on, significant method inlining may occur. This strategy is a variation of *reduce dynamic binding*.

Note that a compiler can not inline virtual methods—those for which it perceives a dynamic binding possibility. To inline, a compiler must statically resolve the particular method at compile time.

An exception to this is HotSpot, which dynamically profiles the running application and can make informed decisions about what to inline. If HotSpot identifies a so-called virtual method *foo* that has only one implementation loaded in the JVM, it may still inline it into method *bar*. In this error-prone case, HotSpot maintains information on these unreliable methods (i.e., *bar* is taking a risk because it inlines a virtual method *foo*). If later on another class is loaded with a second polymorphic implementation of the method *foo* that may require dynamic binding, HotSpot will back out and recompile the method *bar* without inlining *foo*.

Since final, static, and private methods are not virtual, maximizing their declaration provides a helpful hint to the compiler to allow it to inline such methods.

Declaring a class as *final* is a very convenient way to promote inlining, since all methods of a final class are implicitly final. Naturally, a fault with this is that it reduces class extension and reusability, but it is not difficult to "unfinalize" a class.

Note that it is not possible to inline a synchronized method, because of the locking behavior that must be provided. This is one of the indirect ways that synchronized methods affect performance.

In addition to HotSpot, an optimizing JIT compiler can in theory also perform inlining. However, the JIT JVM must trade-off aggressive optimization at the time of first compiling a method (which slows it down) against the goal of fast method compilation. In contrast to HotSpot, JIT compiling takes place in "user time" when a method is first invoked, so fast compile time is important. HotSpot performs optimizing compilation on a background thread, and thus does not meaningfully affect user time performance with respect to compilation. Over time, as JIT algorithms are tuned and hardware gets faster, the JIT JVM designers will apply increasingly aggressive inlining rules.

There are also commercial bytecode optimizing tools (such as DashO) that optimize your bytecode after it has been compiled. These tools perform a thorough analysis of all the class files in the application and redefine all possible methods final (even when they were originally virtual methods) if the tool realizes the method is not overridden or polymorphically redefined. In this way, these tools can promote method inlining. As previously discussed, this approach is error-prone if you are packaging an application framework in which users of the application may subclass and override virtual methods.

To summarize and expand, several steps are required to achieve widespread inlining:

1. Define as many classes final as possible.

2. For non-final classes, define as many methods final or private as possible, or use a bytecode optimizing tool to redefine methods final.

3. Define potential inlined methods with at most two or three statements. Refactor to create short methods. It is the discretion of the compiler to inline; very short methods are more likely to be inlined.

4. Use synchronized methods judiciously; they can not be inlined.

5. Choose a JVM or static native compiler technology that does aggressive inlining, such as HotSpot.

To Compile-time Inline, or Not?

Java bytecode compilers provide an "optimize" option, which allows the compiler, at bytecode generation time, to inline *intra*-class non-virtual methods (methods of class X calling other methods of class X). For intra-class inlining with the Sun javac v1.2 compiler:

```
>javac -O *.java
```

In addition, *inter*-class method inlining can be requested with a special option. For *inter*-class and intra-class inlining with the Sun javac compiler, use the undocumented experimental option *-Xinterclass* on a set of classes:

```
>javac -Xinterclass *.java
```

There is no documentation on the inter-class inlining rules of *javac -Xinterclass*. Disassembling has shown that small inter-class *static* method invocations, and intra-class private method calls are definitely inlined. However, we were not able to coax *javac* to inter-class inline any small, public, final methods of other classes, which indicates that its inlining rules are not very aggressive.

Regardless of the effects of javac optimizing options, we do *not* recommend their use at bytecode compile time, especially for inter-class inlining. By using HotSpot, or similar adaptive optimizing native compilation technologies, the JVM can itself decide on the most appropriate inlining at native compile time, regardless of the inlining choices made at bytecode compile time.

Another reason to avoid inter-class inlining at bytecode compile time is that it can lead to development complications. If a library method was inlined, and then the library changes, the method in which the inlined code resides is now semantically invalid, although nothing and no one is going to tell you that—until the code breaks at run-time.

PROGRAM TO THE JAVA COLLECTION INTERFACES, NOT CLASSES

Java 2 includes the Collections Framework; use it, or the ObjectSpace JGL collections. Declare all your collection objects in terms of the Collection interfaces (for example, *java.util.List* or *Map*), rather than concrete classes, so that it is easy to swap implementations (standard or custom) to experiment with better performers.

The Collection Framework implementation classes (*ArrayList, HashMap, ...*) are the future focus of Sun's efforts at optimization. In addition, there is a reasonable chance that we will see parameterized type Collection classes (like C++ templatized classes) in a future release of the Java Collection Framework; these will provide further performance enhancements[1].

```
// MORE FLEXIBLE; can try faster implementations

List names = new ArrayList();
Iterator iter = names.iterator();


// LESS FLEXIBLE

ArrayList names = new ArrayList();

Vector names = new Vector() ;
Enumeration enum = names.elements();
```

CHOOSE THE BEST COLLECTION

The Java 2 Collection or ObjectSpace JGL libraries provide a much richer set of collection classes than was previously available in the JDK 1.1. For optimal performance, we should choose the appropriate class. Here are some examples:

- Use *LinkedList* instead of *ArrayList* if there is frequent insertion and deletion of elements in the middle or beginning of the list.

- Use a *HashSet* if the purpose of the collection is to test for membership of an object in a set.

Figure 2.1 illustrates a complete decision tree for the implementations in the Collections Framework. This will point you towards the best performing collection for your application's needs.

---

1. Some Sun Java 2 v1.2 Collection Framework documentation hints that parameterized types (like C++ templates) may enter the Java language.

Figure 2.1 Choosing the best performing collection.

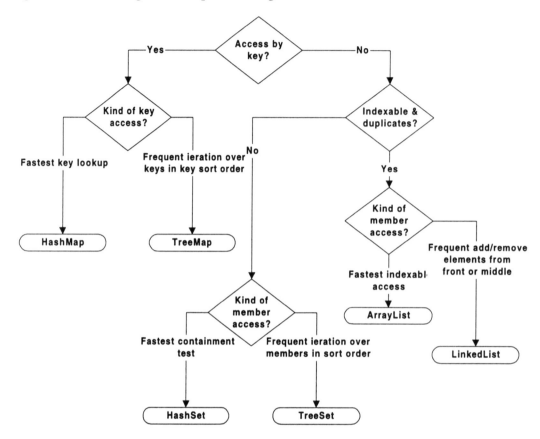

For various algorithms, such as searching and sorting, note that the *Collections* class contains a set of static methods with efficient implementations. For example, *Collections.binarySearch(List, Object)* is an efficient binary search implementation that works quickest on pre-sorted *List* collections.

PRE-SIZE COLLECTIONS

The coding pattern **Hypoth-A-Sized Collection** [PLOP 1997] advises to specify a realistic initial size of a collection when it is created, to avoid the cost of dynamic growing. Suppose, for example, that an *ArrayList* is initially allocated with an array of ten elements. When the eleventh member is added, the object must allocate a new array (perhaps of size 20), copy the ten elements into the new array, and discard the old array. Thus, constant growing requires slow object creation and copying, and the overhead of more garbage collection. And on the other hand, if the realistic size is much *less* than the default, specifying a smaller size can save space and object creation overhead.

Some details:

ArrayList—The default size is 10 elements; this is often too small.

```
  // FASTER, if going to be big
List names = new ArrayList( 1000 );
  // SLOWER
List names = new ArrayList();
```

HashMap—It can be constructed with two factors that influence its performance:

- **initial capacity**—the number of buckets; the default is 101 buckets (although 89 is a preferred value). This value should be a prime number to help minimize collisions when a hash code is reduced to a bucket number.

- **load factor**—percentage fullness of the collection before its capacity is automatically increased (default is 0.75, which is usually adequate).

Higher capacity and lower load factors will tend to improve the search performance, at the expense of increased space. For your workhorse *HashMaps*, experiment with different values, and profile the search performance under realistic load conditions.

```
  // FASTER, assuming we expect 1000-2000 elements.
Map nodes = new HashMap( 1439 );

  // SMALLER, assuming we expect 5 or 10 elements (default is 101 buckets).
Map nodes = new HashMap( 7 );

  // SLOWER
Map nodes = new HashMap();
```

USE CUSTOM COLLECTION IMPLEMENTATIONS

Since the new Java Collections framework is based on interfaces, it is easy to plug in new implementations without affecting your existing client code. The online Sun "Collections trail" tutorial (hyperlinked from the standard SDK documentation) provides an overview of the implementation details, which we won't repeat here. However, here is an example of how performance could be improved with custom collections:

- **Highly concurrent collections**. The synchronization wrappers lock the entire collection (such as *HashMap*), which reduces concurrency. A new hashed collection implementation of *Map* could be defined that only locks on individual buckets. In a multi-threaded application such as a middle-tier server which is constantly using the *Map*, this could remove a significant bottleneck.

USE A LAZY COLLECTION FOR SCROLLING THROUGH LARGE DATASETS

Often a user interface with something like a *JTable* must display a view on to a very large dataset, such as an inventory catalog with millions of elements. The data is retrieved from a database using JDBC, or from a middle-tier server as a serialized collection of objects.

It is not efficient to fetch all the data into memory, so a **lazy collection** (or **lazy model**) is required that encapsulates the logic to perform a lazy fetch of a moderately sized contiguous ranges into the collection.

For example, suppose that initially 1,000 elements are loaded. When the user scrolls (in the *JTable*) beyond the loaded limit—meaning the associated *TableModel.getValueAt(rowIndex, columnIndex)* request refers to a row not in local memory—then a *LargeTableModel* implementation (or the backing lazy collection it is using) requests another 1,000 elements from the remote data source.

In this scenario, the user will experience a pause when they hit a "fault-in" boundary. A variation that may reduce this pause is to use another strategy described earlier, *Exploit Idle Processor Time with Background Future Evaluation*, in which the next block of data is anticipated and loaded on a background thread while the user is looking at a previous block.

Another optimization in this technique is to maintain a most-recently-used (MRU) list of loaded blocks of data. If memory is short, the oldest blocks can be released, and perhaps cached in a local file for subsequent recall. In Java 2, one technique to implement this is to use **reference objects**, which in general are applicable for creating MRU lists or caches which automatically flush when memory is low. For example, consider the *SoftReference* class. Instances of this class hold on to "referents" (other objects). If the JVM is low on memory, the referents are released and garbage collected, at the discretion of the JVM.

Yet another variation on this technique is to exploit idle processor time and prefetch the next block (on a background thread) even before it is requested, in anticipation of its likely use.

OPTIMIZE HASH COLLECTIONS

Hash collections are keyed collections that use hashing (*java.util.Hashtable, java.util.HashMap, java.util.HashSet*, or ObjectSpace's JGL *HashMap* and *HashSet*).

They can in principle provide excellent search performance. But in order to achieve their potential it is important that the hash collection size and hash function be designed to produce an even distribution across the hash collection buckets so that collisions are minimized and so that "clustering" of many keys into one bucket is avoided. It is also important that the frequently invoked *hashCode* and *equals* methods be fast.

Optimize Hash Collections—Avoid String Keys

When you profile a Java application that regularly uses hash collections (e.g., *Hash-Map*, *HashSet*) with *String* objects as keys (which is true of many applications) it is quite likely that you will see an inordinate amount of time spent in the *hashCode* and *equals* methods of *String* objects. An inspection of the *get* method in the *HashMap* class reveals what is going on.

```
// class HashMap
public Object get( Object key )
{
  Entry tab[] = table;

  if ( key != null )
  {
    int hash = key.hashCode();

    // ...

    if ( e.hash == hash && key.equals(e.key) )
      return e.value;

    // ...
```

Every time the *get* method is invoked, the *hashCode* method on the parameter *key* is invoked, and the *equals* method is invoked for each object in the cluster chain. Unfortunately, the Sun programmers of the *String* class did not make the *hashCode* method return a cached value—rather, it is recalculated each time (Listing 2.1). It is an undesirable performance hit for such a workhorse method in an immutable object—the advice to cache reusable things was not followed.[1]

---

1. Perhaps to avoid the extra int field required in each string?

Listing 2.1 A portion of a common *String.hashCode* implementation.

```
public int hashCode()
{
  // declarations ...

  if ( len < 16 )
  {
    for ( int i = len ; i > 0; i-- )
      h = (h * 37) + val[off++];
  } else
       // ...
```

So what are some better alternatives? Here are several:

- Use *Integer* objects as keys. The *hashCode* method simply returns the stored primitive *int* value, and the *equals* test just compares the *int* values. These are fast methods.

- Use a wrapper *Key* class around a string that caches the string's hash code in an instance variable. Benchmarks show that this simple improvement *cuts in half* the time to execute the *HashMap.get* method. See Listing 2.2.

Listing 2.2 The Key class is faster than a String as a hash key.

```
public final class Key
{
  private String    key;
  private int       hashCode;

  public Key( String key )
  {
    setKey( key );
  }

  public void setKey( String key )
  {
    this.key = key;
    hashCode = key.hashCode();
  }

    // caching the hash code speeds lookup

  public int hashCode()
  {
    return hashCode;
  }
}
```

```
public boolean equals( Object object )
{
  if ( this == object )
    return true;
  else if ( object == null || getClass() != object.getClass() )
    return false;

  Key other = (Key) object;
  return key.equals( other.key );
}
}
```

```
  // FASTER lookup

Map nodes = new HashMap( 89 );
...
Key key = new Key( name );
...
nodes.put( key, node );


  // SLOWER

Map nodes = new HashMap( 89 );
...
nodes.put( name, node );
```

Optimize Hash Collections—Prime Size

G. H. Hardy, the great British number theorist who worked with prime numbers, among many other things, happily claimed "No discovery of mine has made, or is likely to make...the least difference to the amenity of the world." Little did he know that prime numbers would acquire prominence in encryption—and in hash collections. Some advice:

■ Define the size of the hash collection to be a prime number; this tends to avoid clustering. Definitely avoid the size of the table being a power of two (64, 128, ...). These values strongly promote clustering.

- Initialize small hash collections that you predict are going to hold around 100 to 200 elements to an original size of 89 (a prime number). If you expect your *java.util* hash collection to grow dynamically, be aware that the default growth factor formula is 2n + 1. So we would like to pick an initial size that continues generating a series of prime numbers for the table size as it grows. It turns out that an excellent choice for the starting size in this case is the number 89. Unfortunately, the Sun programmers of the *Hashtable* and *HashMap* classes chose an original size of 101 rather than 89; 101 does not exhibit a desirable growth pattern in terms of generating a series of prime numbers.

Here is a list of some prime numbers to consider for the initial bucket size:

89, 179, 359, 719, 1439, 2879, 11519, 23039, 737279, 1474559, 2949119

```
// FASTER, if going to grow

Map nodes = new HashMap( 89 );


// SLOWER. defaults to 101

Map nodes = new HashMap();
```

Optimize Hash Collections—Good Hash Function

The *hashCode* method should produce an even distribution across the hash collection buckets so that collisions are minimized and so that "clustering" of many keys in one bucket is avoided.

- **Override the inherited** *Object.hashCode* **method,** for objects that are to be hash collection keys. The default implementation returns the object reference value; these do not exhibit an even distribution.

- **Understand the distribution characteristics of the keys for the hashCode method, and avoid bias.** A good hash code should produce a positive integer that is evenly distributed across a large range. The code is usually in part a function of the underlying data or keys. If the underlying data is skewed or biased, this can influence the hash code to not be evenly distributed.

There has been successful work in defining a general-purpose hash function algorithm that is independent of the key characteristics. We recommend you consider defining the Pearson [Pearson 1990] or Uzgalis [Uzgalis 1991] general-purpose hash algorithms in Java (see http://serve.net/buz/hash.adt/java.000.html).

USE EXTERNALIZABLE RATHER THAN SERIALIZABLE

In Java 2, even for very simple classes such as is shown in Listing 2.3 (the requisite exception handling has been removed for brevity), defining your own implementation of *Externalizable* is at least *four times faster* than *Serializable*.

For more complex object structures that involve the serialization of deep object graphs, the performance of custom control with *Externalizable* grows even larger. We know of examples where performance was ten times better with *Externalizable*.

This performance gain will best be enjoyed during remote method invocation, using either RMI or ObjectSpace Voyager, with the serialization of return values and parameters.

Listing 2.3 Sample Externalizable and Serializable timing tests.

```
// SLOWER

public class TestSerial implements Serializable
{
  private String attr1;
  private int    attr2;
}


// FASTER

public class TestExternal implements Externalizable
{
  private String attr1;
  private int    attr2;

  public void readExternal( ObjectInput s )
  {
    attr1 = (String) s.readObject();
    attr2 = s.readInt();
  }
```

```
public void writeExternal( ObjectOutput s )
{
    s.writeObject( attr1 );
    s.writeInt( attr2 );
}
}
```

USE STRINGBUFFER.APPEND RATHER THAN STRING CONCATENATION

The following design using string concatenation is undesirable:

```
// SLOWER

String s = "foo";

for ( int i = 0; i < max; i++ )
{
    s += stringArray[ i ];
}
```

This is because a new *String* (and *StringBuffer)* instance is created and assigned to s for each concatenation; each old String s released for garbage collection (internally, *StringBuffer.append* and *toString* are used in the concatenation). Bear in mind that strings are immutable, so any modification (such as concatenation) involves creation of a new *String* and a new *StringBuffer*.

This leads to the usual ills of excessive short-lived object creation described in the previous chapter. In general, designs applying string concatenation may suffer from excessive implicit intermediate string creation and release.

The better-performing solution is to concatenate with one explicit *StringBuffer* instance, using *append* messages.

In addition, the initial default internal character array buffer size of a *StringBuffer* is 16, which is usually too small. When the buffer is full, a new buffer twice the size of the original is created (for example, 32), the old buffer is copied, and then released.

This can reintroduce the kind of implicit repeated object creation/release we are trying to avoid.

Therefore, it is advisable to construct the *StringBuffer* with an initial buffer size equal to the approximate maximum required.

```
// FASTER; assumes we know 200 is a good approximation of the maximum length

StringBuffer buffer = new StringBuffer( 200 );
buffer.append( "foo" );

for ( int i = 0; i < max; i++ )
{
  buffer.append( stringArray[ i ] );
}

String newString = buffer.toString();
```

Note that *StringBuffer.append* returns the *StringBuffer* instance, so we can cascade the append calls. Consequently, the following style provides an approximation of the desirable succinctness of the "+" operator.

```
StringBuffer buffer = new StringBuffer( 400 ).append( s1 ).append( s2 );

... // do other work to get s3, s4, and s5

String newString = buffer.append( s3 ).append( s4 ).append( s5 ).toString();
```

DO STRING MANIPULATION IN A STRINGBUFFER

Starting in Java 2, the *StringBuffer* class includes operations to replace, delete, and insert characters in the *StringBuffer* instance. In contrast, if using *String* objects, these operations cause the inefficient generation of many new *String* objects, since strings are immutable.

USE REPEATED STRING OPERATOR "+" IN ONE STATEMENT

Consider the following string concatenation statement:

```
// FASTER

String s = s1 + "cat" + s2 + "dog";
```

The Sun Java 2 compiler will transform this into the equivalent efficient expression using *StringBuffer*:

```
String s = new StringBuffer( ).append( s1 ).append( "cat" ).
                        append( s2 ).append( "dog" ).toString();
```

Therefore, the example making repeated use of operator "+" in one statement is very efficient, with the small exception of the *StringBuffer* being initialized with an inadequate size of 16, which is not a significant problem if we know the total length will be small.

However, if the first expression were rewritten into multiple statements, several temporary intermediate *String* objects will be created and released, which is undesirable.

```
// SLOWER

String s = new String();
s = s + s1;
s = s + "cat";
s = s + s2;
s = s + "dog";
```

DO NOT REUSE A STRINGBUFFER FOR MANY STRING MANIPULATIONS

So I think I'll be smart and optimize my "little language" parser and interpreter subsystem. I avoid object creation by just making one long-lived workhorse instance of a StringBuffer, which I use repeatedly, resetting its length to 0 as needed. I know that *buffer.setLength(0)* has the effect that a subsequent *buffer.toString* returns an empty string. I think this shrinks the internal character array buffer down to a nice small starting size again. Wrong.

What I didn't know was this:

```
// newString and buffer share the same internal
// character array, for better speed and space performance

String newString = buffer.toString();
```

And I didn't know this:

```
// Step 1: The shared internal character array is copied.
// Step 2: buffer points to the new array;
//         newString points to the old array.
// Step 3: Each element of the new array is assigned a null character.

buffer.setLength( 0 );
```

This is known as copy-on-change behavior, and it allows objects to share representations (such as character arrays) until one of the objects changes its representation.

The very unpleasant implications of these facts are seen in the following scenario.

```
// Suppose the StringBuffer and String share a
// (pretty big) 5,000-element character array.

String s1 = buffer.toString();


// A second 5,000-element array is now created.
```

```
// s1 points to the first array; buffer points to the second.

buffer.setLength( 0 );


// buffer only contains 6 relevant characters, but its array is size 5,000

buffer.append( "cat" );
...
buffer.append( "dog" );


// s2 and buffer share the second 5,000-element array

String s2 = buffer.toString();


// Oh no! Grotesque memory wastage...
// A third 5,000-element array is created.
// s2 points to the second 5,000-element array; buffer points to the third.

buffer.setLength( 0 );
```

Hopefully you can see the problems:

■ The first invocation of *buffer.setLength(0)* makes a new array of size 5,000; perhaps it didn't need to be that big. A *StringBuffer's* internal character array never shrinks in size.

■ The string s2 contains a 5,000-element character array, even though it only contains the 6 characters "catdog." If I continue to use the same buffer object, each time I execute *aString=buffer.toString*, and then *buffer.setLength(0)*, then each string will have another 5,000-element array, no matter how few characters there are in it.

The moral of this story: Throw away your used *StringBuffers*, and create new ones.

OPTIMIZING LOOPS

Optimizing Loops—Move Loop Invariants

Loop invariants should be moved outside of loops (also known as "loop invariant code motion"). It has two advantages:

1. Eliminates unnecessary duplicate work.

2. Java compilers usually try to store local variables in processor registers, which provides especially fast access. If loop invariants are assigned to local variables, this fact can be exploited.

Moving loop invariants usually has only minor impact on performance, but in numerically intensive algorithms such as those related to graphics and simulation (involving lots of looping) it can have moderate impact.

For example:

```
// FASTER
int count = policy.getVehicleCount();
IAddress address = company.getAddress();

for ( int i = 0; i < count; i++ )
{
   ... address ...
}


// SLOWER
for ( int i = 0; i < policy.getVehicleCount(); i++ )
{
   ... company.getAddress() ...
}
```

An optimizing compiler is able to automatically identify and move some invariants outside of the loop, but this is not possible in all cases. Thus, it is more reliable to explicitly code this, if performance at the loop is a hotspot.

At times the loop invariant is not so obvious. In a nested loop, references may be invariant in the inner loop, but not the outer. For example:

```
// FASTER

Person p;

for ( int i = 0; i < maxI; i++ )
{
☛   p = persons.get( i );

  for ( int j = 0; j < maxJ; j++ )
   {
☛    ... p ...  // persons.get( i ) is invariant in the inner loop
   }
}


  // SLOWER

for ( int i = 0; i < maxI; i++ )
{
  for ( int j = 0; j < maxJ; j++ )
   {
☛    ... persons.get( i ) ...
   }
}
```

Optimizing Loops—Unroll Loops

For some loops, the overhead of the loop management is a significant percentage of the overall loop cost, because the operation is simple. In this case, to reduce the cost of loop management, try loop expansion (loop unrolling).

```
// FASTER
for ( int i = array.length - 1; i > 10; i -= 10 )
{
  array[ i ] = array[ i - 1 ] + array[ i - 2 ];
  array[ i - 1 ] = array[ i - 2 ] + array[ i - 3 ];
  array[ i - 2 ] = array[ i - 3 ] + array[ i - 4 ];
  // ...
  array[ i - 9 ] = array[ i - 10 ] + array[ i - 11 ];
}


  // SLOWER
for (int i = array.length - 1; i > 1; i-- )
{
  array[ i ] = array[ i - 1 ] + array[ i - 2 ];
}
```

Loop unrolling is actually an example of the more high-level general performance strategy of "do more work in each step, when the overhead of each step is high."

Optimizing Loops—Unswitch It

Sometimes a loop contains case logic in this pattern:

```
// SLOWER
for (int i = 0; i > max; i++ )
{
  if ( code.equals( "red" ) )
  {
    // do X
```

```
   }
   else
   {
     // do Y
   }
}
```

Note that the value of code is a loop invariant. Therefore, it is possible to unswitch the loop and perform the test outside. It can be rewritten as:

```
   // FASTER
if ( code.equals( "red" ) )
{
   for (int i = 0; i > max; i++ )
   {
     // do X
   }
}
else
{
   for (int i = 0; i > max; i++ )
   {
     // do Y
   }
}
```

Like most low-level code rewrites to improve performance, the gain in performance is at the expense of awkward code.

OPTIMIZE APPLETS—USE JAR FILES

To reduce the applet class loading overhead on a network, bundle the resources required by an applet (classes, images, and so on) into a JAR file. This is a widely described technique, so it will not be elaborated here. This is a specialization of *do more in one step, when the overhead of each step is expensive*, and was mentioned in the previous chapter. And as described previously, compression of the JAR file can be further enhanced by using a bytecode optimizing tool that minimizes the size of each bytecode file.

USE BUFFERED I/O

The *BufferedOutputStream, BufferedWriter* and related classes should be used to provide efficient writing and reading of data. In general, they should wrap an inner *Stream* or *Writer* whose operations are slow/costly, such as files and possibly sockets. It is best if the buffered stream directly wraps the slow source or sink of data—for example, the *BufferedWriter* should directly wrap a *FileWriter*, rather than wrap another writer which wraps a *FileWriter*. In addition, for optimal I/O the default buffer size (which is a char array of size 8192 for *BufferedWriter*, for example) may need to be overridden—bigger is usually better.

```
// FASTER

PrintWriter writer = new PrintWriter(
    new BufferedWriter( new FileWriter( "data.out" ) ) ) ;

// SLOWER

PrintWriter writer = new PrintWriter( ( new FileWriter( "data.out" ) ) );
```

ON OLDER JVMS, REDUCE THE USE OF SYNCHRONIZED METHODS

The best and latest native compilers and optimized JVMs do not impose any significant lock management overhead to invoke synchronized methods. A sample of synchronization-optimized JVMs includes:

- Sun Java 2 v1.2 JIT JVM

- Sun HotSpot JVM

Other, or older, JVMs may impose some lock overhead on a synchronized method call. Of course, the best solution is to upgrade the JVM. Failing that, design to avoid invoking synchronized methods.

Although modern JVMs do not impose a lock management penalty for synchronized methods, they still can cause other performance and design problems. This includes deadlock problems, "serialized" execution one thread at a time (reducing concurrency), and the inability to inline synchronized methods when the compiler is performing optimizations.

Some techniques to avoid synchronization include:

- Increase the use of **immutable objects** (read-only objects) that do not require synchronization. Class *String* is the quintessential example of an immutable object.

- Try to avoid synchronizing private methods; synchronize only public methods that have concurrency problems. Then, if a call acquires the object lock via a public method *m1*, *m1* can safely call the unsynchronized private methods without fear of concurrency problems (since it will be the only thread of control in unsafe aspects of the object). Of course, the calls to the unsynchronized private methods will be faster since no lock acquire/release is required, and the private method may even be inlined (any synchronized method can not be inlined).

- Use the *Double-Checked Locking* pattern (described in the chapter on concurrency idioms) to lock only for rarely entered critical sections.

REDUCE OBJECT SIZE AND CREATION WITH WEAK TYPING AND THE INSTANCEOF OPERATOR

This (paraphrased) example comes from the *Sun JDC Tech Tips* (Dec. 16, 1997).

An application was required that created a very large (millions of bytes) abstract syntax tree structure from parsing a large Java program. Non-leaf nodes contained child nodes, but no string information, while leaf nodes had no children, but do contain string information. The nodes in the tree were first represented like this:

```
public class Node
{
  private int type;
  private Node children[];
  private String info;
  // ...
}
```

Since every byte counted in this memory-hungry application, there were three defects with this design:

1. The use of *children* or *info* is mutually exclusive; one of the fields was wasted.

2. It was discovered that most of the time (95%) there was only one child node. The storage overhead of an array (which maintains dimension information) was usually wasteful.

3. The type could be dynamically derived, it did not need to be cached in an *int*.

The JDC-described solution (an alternative is described later) was to use a single attribute of type *Object* (**weak typing**) to stand for the *String*, single child *Node*, or an array of *Nodes*; note that an *Object[]* can bind to a variable declared as type *Object*. Then, methods such as the *getChild* method use the *instanceof* operator to determine the type of node. See Listing 2.4.

Listing 2.4 A memory-optimized Node class.

```
public final class Node
{
  private Object data;

  // constructors, etc. ...


  /**
   * Return the i-th child
   */
  public Node getChild( int i )
  {
      // most common case

    if ( isLeaf() )
      return null;
```

```
  // data is instanceof Node
else if ( i == 1 )
  return (Node) data;

  // i >= 2

else
  return ( (Node[]) data )[ i - 2 ];
}


public boolean isLeaf()
{
  return data instanceof String;
}
}
```

Note the rather subtle optimization of being able to avoid using an array when a non-leaf node has only one child. If a one-child node has a second child added to it, an array is created and both children are placed in it. This design trades off speed for space.

In this way, the use of variables declared simply of type *Object* and the *instanceof* operator can be applied to reduce the size of objects, and the number of objects that need to be created.

LAZY INITIALIZATION

There are many situations when a field or collection of elements may not need to immediately (or perhaps ever) be initialized. If initialization requires complex logic or is expensive, such as requiring lots of object creation, remote communication, or involves grabbing an "expensive" resource such as a database connection, then *Lazy Initialization* can be applied [Beck 1997].

A common implementation of lazy initialization is in an accessing method for a field. The method tests for a distinguished value (usually null) and initializes the field if necessary.

The key requirement of lazy initialization of properties is that an accessing method is always used for access to the logical property—both internally and of course externally. This is quite feasible for JavaBeans properties, which require a public accessing method.

Listing 2.5 Lazy initialization in an accessing method.

```
public class Foo
{
  private A a;
  private B b;

  public A getA()
  {
    if ( a == null )
      a = new A();

    return a;
  }

  // ...
}
```

Lazy Initialization in Singleton Methods

In a *Singleton* method [GHJV 1995] it is fairly common to initialize the singleton when the field is declared, as in Listing 2.6.

Listing 2.6 Typical singleton initialization.

```
public class Foo
{
➤ private static Foo instance = new Foo();

  public static Foo getInstance()
  {
    return instance;
  }

  // ...
}
```

However, lazy initialization is also common. It is advantageous if the constructor requires exception handling or creating the object is "expensive" or slow in some way (such as in acquiring another resource). See Listing 2.7. Note that the method is synchronized to avoid a race condition in the initialization section. A minor variation on this is to use the *Double-Checked Locking* pattern (described in the chapter on concurrency idioms).

Listing 2.7 Lazy initialization in a Singleton method.

```
public class Foo
{
  private static Foo instance;

  public static synchronized Foo getInstance()
  {
    if ( instance == null )
      instance = new Foo();

    return instance;
  }

  // ...
}
```

Lazy Initialization of EJB Properties

The growing popularity of Enterprise JavaBeans (EJB), combined with the expense of obtaining a remote reference to another EJB object motivates the use of lazy initialization in EJB applications.

For example, assume "bean-managed persistence" is used in an *EntityBean* (this example could also apply to a stateful *SessionBean*). If *Account* is an entity bean, and it has an association with a *Customer*, which is also an entity bean, then the accessing method in *Account* may lazy initialize the instance field reference to the *Customer*, since it is an expensive operation. Listing 2.8 illustrates the idea.

By the way, a future generation of "container-managed persistence" entity beans will obviate the need for this particular use of lazy initialization, but we suspect that there will still be plenty of opportunities to handcraft lazy initialization of remote references.

Listing 2.8 Lazy initialization of EJB remote references.

```
public class Account implements javax.ejb.EntityBean
{
  private ICustomer     customer;
  private CustomerKey   customerKey;
  // ...

  public ICustomer getCustomer() throws RemoteException
  {
    ICustomerHome    home = null;

    if ( customer == null )
    {
      try
      {
        // typical EJB: use JNDI and the EJB Home object
        // to obtain a remote reference to another entity bean

        home = (ICustomerHome) jndiContext.lookup( CUSTOMER_HOME_NAME );
        customer = home.findByPrimaryKey( customerKey );
      }
      catch ( Exception ex )
      {
        // ...
      }
    }

    return customer;
  }

  // ...
}
```

CONSIDER A HIGH-PERFORMANCE ASCIISTRING CLASS

Some Java applications spend an extraordinary amount of time in *String* methods such as *equals, getBytes,* and *hashCode*. This is especially true of server-side applications that handle string-based network protocols such as HTTP and SMTP. Note that these protocols are ASCII string-based. Note also that *java.lang.String* is encoded with 2-byte Unicode characters (type *char* in Java), the *hashCode* method is non-optimal because hash codes are not cached (as previously discussed), and ASCII/Unicode conversion operations involve (rather expensive) collaboration with a subclass of *sun.io.CharToByteConverter*.

The point is that there is significant overhead with *java.lang.String* that is unnecessary and inefficient when ASCII-specific string protocols are being handled—there is continual conversion going on between ASCII bytes and the Unicode *char* type.

If profiling reveals that the use of *String* is consuming an inordinate amount of time in this context, then we suggest creating a replacement class for *String*. We recommend a high-performance lightweight *AsciiString* class that caches its hash code, and—most significantly—that simply contains an array of type *byte* (ASCII bytes). This is in contrast to *String*, which contains an array of type *char*.

3 IMPROVING PERFORMANCE— MINOR

In this chapter

- Optimization techniques which are likely to make only a minor improvement.

REPLACE SYSTEM.CURRENTTIMEMILLIS WITH A CLOCK

System.currentTimeMillis is not blinding fast, so if an application invokes this operation frequently, performance will suffer slightly. If second-level time granularity is sufficient for an application (which is often the case), then use a *Clock* (a *"Sleepy-Clock"*) that only calls *System.currentTimeMillis* once per second (and then sleeps), and caches the time.

A timing test showed that 1 million calls to *System.currentTimeMillis* took approximately 80,000 milliseconds, but took only 60 milliseconds for *Clock.getTime*—a very significant improvement.

This technique can be viewed as a specialization of *cache reusable things*. See Listing 3.1.

Listing 3.1 A "sleepy" Clock

```
public final class Clock implements Runnable
{
  private long    time = System.currentTimeMillis();
  private int     sleepTime;
  private Thread thread;

  public Clock( int sleepTime )
  {
    this.sleepTime = sleepTime;
    thread = new Thread( this );
    thread.start();
  }

  public long getTime()
  {
    return time;
  }

  public void run()
  {
    if ( Thread.currentThread() != thread )
      return;

    while ( true )
    {
      try
      {
        Thread.sleep( sleepTime );
        time = System.currentTimeMillis();
      }
      catch( Exception ex )
      {
        ex.printStackTrace();
      }
    }
  }
}
```

Another mechanism for efficient timing is to use the new Java 2 *javax.swing.Timer* that sleeps for a regular interval, and then wakes up and emits an *ActionEvent* to *ActionListeners*, using the delegation event model.

CONSIDER A BYTECODE OPTIMIZER

There are commercial third-party tools, such as DashO, that optimize the bytecode files generated by a Java compiler. The main optimization is reduction in size of a set of bytecode files; a 30% reduction in JAR file size is not uncommon. These tools also obfuscate the code, which is in fact one of the mechanisms by which the file size is reduced, because the obfuscated names are typically shorter.

Naturally, this improves load time when class loading—especially important if loading over a network, such as in an applet. It will create a micro-improvement in the speed of bytecode verification (if active), since there are fewer codes. To reduce bytecode file size, these products remove all unused classes, methods, constant-pool entries, and fields, based upon a dependency trace rooted at a user-specified method, such as a particular *main*.

These products can also help slightly with run-time performance. For example, they will "devirtualize" methods (i.e., declare them as *final*) that are discovered to never be overridden. This makes it possible for JIT compilers or HotSpot to inline methods which could not otherwise be easily inlined.

If the optimizer does perform devirtualizing, note that this approach is error-prone if you are packaging an application framework in which users of the application may subclass and extend the framework. The optimizer may have incorrectly devirtualized methods that should have remained virtual to properly enable subclass overriding.

Avoid Initialization If Constructors Assign to Fields

In general, initializing a field where it is declared is desirable because it makes it easier to understand the nature and role of the field—the reader need only read the declaration line. If the reader has to scan one or more constructors to determine the field value, then the code is unnecessarily complex. Thus, the following is common in Java:

```
public class Node
{
  private String name = "i am a node";

  // ...
}
```

However, if a constructor is normally used to assign to a field, via a constructor, then the original field initialization is a wasteful step that creates a very short lived object. In this case, the field should be left uninitialized, as in:

```
public class Node
{
  private String name;

  public Node( String name )
  {
    this.name = name;
  }

  // ...
}
```

WORK WITH INTERFACES RATHER THAN CLASSES

Some older, well-meaning Java performance literature suggests that casting to a class is faster than casting to an interface. Similar claims have been made that it is faster to invoke methods on a variable declared in terms of a class rather than an interface. However, benchmarking with modern JVMs and native compilers indicates no significant difference.

Therefore, from a performance perspective it is preferable to cast to interfaces and use "interface" variables because it allows us to easily try different implementations of interfaces that may exhibit better performance, without having to change the client source code that uses the interfaces.

A good example of this strategy is using the Collections Framework interfaces such as *List* and *Map*. By programming to the interfaces, new implementations with different performance characteristics can be painlessly introduced.

ORDER TESTS BY FREQUENCY

This is a specific example of the high-level performance strategy of *exploit patterns in the data*. Organize compound tests and if-else structures so that a test is resolved as soon as possible based on a comprehension of the patterns in the data. In other words, test the common things first.

```java
public void foo( String code )
{
   if ( code.equals( "most common" ) )
   {
     // ...
   } else if ( code.equals( "second" ) )
   {
     // ...
   } else if ( code.equals( "third" ) )
   {
     // ...
   }
}
```

Note that this advice can be ignored for *switch* statements, because the switch operation uses an efficient table lookup; the order of cases in a switch does not degrade performance.

USE ARRAYS INSTEAD OF COLLECTIONS

Warning: This is not as helpful as it sounds. Accessing array elements is two to three times faster than using collection objects such as *ArrayList*. If the size is known and fixed, and elements can be indexed by integers, using an array will *very slightly* improve performance (see next paragraph). And fortunately, be aware than in Java

2 there is a helper utility class for common array algorithms (searching, sorting, …): *java.util.Arrays*.

However, although three times faster sounds impressive, timing tests show that array access is *very* fast. So three times a profoundly small number is still a very small number. In other words, both arrays and *ArrayList* are very fast.

As an experiment, we executed a test one million times for both an array and for an *ArrayList* object (both with 500 elements) that retrieved and replaced an element, and which iterated over all the elements (using an *Iterator* for the *ArrayList*). Please see Listing 3.2.

Listing 3.2 Timing test using an array versus ArrayList.

```
public static void testArrayVersusList()
{
  int keyCount    = 500;
  int loopCount   = 1000000;

  Set s           = Key.getSampleKeys( keyCount );
  List l          = new ArrayList( s );
  Object[] array  = l.toArray();
  List list       = Arrays.asList( array );


    // array test

  long t1 = System.currentTimeMillis();
  System.out.println( "start testing array at " + t1 );

  for ( int i = 0; i < loopCount; i++ )
  {
    Key key = (Key) array[ i % keyCount  ];
    array[ i % keyCount  ] = key;

    for ( int j = 0; j < array.length; j++ )
    {
      Key key2 = (Key) array[ j % keyCount  ];
    }

  }

  long t2 = System.currentTimeMillis();
  System.out.println( "end " + t2 + " . diff = " + ( t2 - t1 )  );


    // list test
```

```
t1 = System.currentTimeMillis();
System.out.println( "start testing List at " + t1 );

for ( int i = 0; i < loopCount; i++ )
{
  Key key = (Key) list.get( i % keyCount  );
  list.set( i % keyCount, key );

  for ( Iterator j = list.iterator(); j.hasNext(); )
  {
    Key key2 = (Key) j.next();
  }

}

t2 = System.currentTimeMillis();
System.out.println( "end " + t2 + " . diff = " + ( t2 - t1 )  );
}
```

For a plain array, it took roughly only one minute, and for the *ArrayList*, roughly three minutes. One million times is a very significant amount of repetition, implying that it really takes a lot of work before any meaningful measurable difference arises. This observation leads to the following advice ...

USE COLLECTIONS INSTEAD OF ARRAYS

The previous section illustrates that *ArrayList* is slower that an array, but not in any really meaningful way, since they are both still very fast.

Given that, there are some advantages to sticking with *List* objects rather than arrays. These include:

- The developer can consistently program and think in terms of *List* objects, instead of sometimes an array, and sometimes a *List*.

- By programming consistently to the *List* interface, there is the possibility to replace the implementation (e.g., *ArrayList*) with other *List* implementations without breaking the client code, and thus experiment with different performance characteristics of various data structures. In short, more flexibility.

Use Double-Checked Locking to Reduce Synchronization

Although modern JVMs considerably reduce the overhead of a synchronized method, if we wish to reduce it still further, or otherwise ensure we limit synchronization only to a critical section, the *Double-Checked Locking* pattern [PLOP 1997] can be used.

Consider the example of a "Singleton" method implementing the *Singleton* pattern [GHJV 1995]. This is likely to be a high-use method, but the critical section is in the rarely entered lazy initialization block. It is not desirable to synchronize the method, when only a very rarely entered block contains the critical section for which the synchronization was required. Synchronizing the entire method adds unnecessary overhead for all method invocations, and reduces concurrency.

We recommend that *Double-Checked Locking* always be applied in the definition of lazy initialized singleton methods, but please note that this technique is not limited to the *Singleton* pattern.

The solution is illustrated in the code sample; the comments explain the details. The big picture is that it is possible to push synchronization into a rarely entered block when the critical section is rarely executed, and to double-check the block-entry condition after synchronization, so that the critical section is not executed redundantly or inappropriately.

Listing 3.3 Double-checked locking Singleton method.

```
// FASTER

public class SharePool
{

private static SharePool instance;

// Un-synched singleton method.

public static SharePool getInstance()
{
    // Rarely entered block. Push synchronization inside it.
    // This is the FIRST CHECK.
```

```
if ( instance == null )
{
  // Only 1 thread at a time gets past the next point.
  // Rarely executed synchronization statement.

  synchronized( SharePool.class )
  {
    // If a second thread was waiting to get here,
    // it will now find that the work has been completed,
    // and it will not re-do the work.
    // This is the DOUBLE CHECK

    if ( instance == null )
    {
      // Here is the critical section that lazy
      // initializes the singleton variable.

      instance = new SharePool();
    }
  }
}
return instance;
}

// ...

} // end of  class
```

Of course, it looks rather long-winded with the comments; the following sample shows it in its typical form, contrasted with its alternative—synchronizing the entire method.

Listing 3.4 Double-checked locking Singleton method, without annotation.

```
// FASTER (without comments)

public static SharePool getInstance()
{
  if ( instance == null )
  {
    synchronized( SharePool.class )
    {
      if ( instance == null )
        instance = new SharePool();
    }
  }
  return instance;
}


  // SLOWER (less concurrency)
```

```
public static synchronized SharePool getInstance()
{
  if ( instance == null )
    instance = new SharePool();
  return instance ;
}
```

OPTIMIZING LOOPS—IGNORE OUTDATED LOOP CONTROL ADVICE

Some well-meaning Java performance literature recommends so-called loop improvements that in theory make sense, but that benchmarking with modern JVMs and native compilers indicate actually reduce performance (although they may have helped on older compilers when the advice was written).

There is a more general lesson in this: Many fine-grained "performance" modifications to code have little or no measurable benefit, either because the benefit is immeasurably slight, or because optimizing compilers will take the initiative to improve the "worse" code. In fact, it is even worse than that: When we try to be clever and make our code convoluted in the name of performance, an optimizing compiler may be defeated (since they look for often-used patterns) and produce even slower results.

With respect to the loop recommendations, we hypothesize this is because compilers have been optimized for the tried-and-true *for (int i = 0 ; i < max ; i++)*. However, even if the alternatives did improve performance, the improvements would tend to be very minimal.

Listing 3.5 Loop constructs.

```
  // FASTER; tried-and-true. Compilers are tuned to
  // recognize and optimize this

for ( int i = 0; i < max; i++ )
{
  // ...
}

// (surprise) SLOWER; counting down, testing 0
```

```
for ( int i = max; --i != 0; )
{
  // ...
}



  // (surprise) SLOWER; avoiding a bounds test
  // may be suitable if the bounds test is complex/expensive

try
{
  for ( int i = 0; ; i++ )
  {
    // ...
  }
}
catch( ArrayOutOfBoundsException ex ) {}
```

TEST FOR SET MEMBERSHIP USING HASHSET

For an algorithm that needs to test if an object is a member of a set, the Java 2 Collections operation *HashSet.contains* is much faster than its alternatives (such as *ArrayList.contains*), especially when the elements are well distributed among the buckets. This is true even for small collections of five or six elements, in contradiction to some advice which (incorrectly) suggested that for very small collections, the linear search in a list would perform better than a hashing algorithm lookup.

See also the previous discussion on using a cached hash code in a *Key* class rather than *String* instances, in order to optimize lookup.

REPLACE RECURSION WITH ITERATION

An algorithm that uses a tail-recursive method will typically take longer than an iterative solution, because of the overhead of the method calls. For example, the following tail-recursive factorial method took on average five times as long as an iterative version.

```
// SLOWER - tail recursive design

public static double recursiveFactorial( int n )
{
    if ( n <= 1 )
        return 1;

    return n * recursiveFactorial( n - 1 );
}
```

USE LOCAL VARIABLES STORED IN REGISTERS

Java compilers will try to allocate the earliest declared local variables to the processor registers, which provide much faster access than fetches from memory. In large loops, this can help slightly.

```
public final void foo( IPolicy policy )
{
    // number probably stored in a register
    int count = policy.getVehicleCount();

    // object reference probably stored in register
    IAddress myAddress = myAddressInstanceVariable;

    for ( int i = 0; i < reallyBigNumber; i++ )
    {
        ... count ...
        ... myAddress ...
    }
}
```

This strategy is most commonly applied to loop invariants.

STRING SEARCH—USE THE ALPHAWORKS STRINGSEARCH CLASS

Fast string searching is possible, but not using the Java 2 v1.2 libraries. Fortunately, IBM has implemented a *StringSearch* class that adds fast string search capabilities to Java 2. If your application is doing intensive string searching, use class *StringSearch* rather than *String.indexOf* or other alternatives.

The IBM alphaWorks website (www.alphaworks.ibm.com) contains many useful, free Java classes, including *com.ibm.jtc.text.StringSearch*.

StringSearch provides fast, internationalized-compliant (Unicode) string search based on the popular Boyer-Moore algorithm, plus some other tricks. It can often achieve performance proportional to (length of text) / (length of pattern), while also avoiding temporary object creation. The JDK 2 library does *not* include a high-performance service based on these techniques. However, Java 2 does include improvements to the *java.text.CollationElementIterator* that provide the basis for using these techniques.

STRENGTH REDUCTION—USE CHEAPER OPERATIONS

Strength reduction occurs by replacing an operation with another that executes faster—perhaps by using fewer bytecode instructions or requiring less work of the processor. A common application of this in Java is to use the compound assignment operators, which will generate less bytecode than their alternatives. Any improvement will be minimal—it is more significant for non-local variables because of the bytecode operations used—but it is painless to use the compound assignment operators, so it is definitely recommended. Here are some examples:

```
// FASTER: uses 1 instruction
total += subtotal;

// SLOWER: uses 5 instruction unless the compiler optimizes
total = total + subtotal;
```

```
// FASTER (shift operator when multiply or divide by powers of 2)
x = y << 1;

// SLOWER
x = y * 2;
```

Another example of strength reduction is to replace *equals* calls with == tests. This is not often possible, but as an example, consider the *String.intern* method.

Calling *String.intern* returns a *String* from a unique pool of *String* constants. Consider the following:

```
// if s1.equals( s2 ) then s1.intern() == s2.intern()

String s1 = new String( "cat" );
String s2 = new String( "cat" );

String internOfS1 = s1.intern();
String internOfS2 = s2.intern();

internOfS1 == internOfS2 --> true
```

If we are creating a design in which a known set of string constants is going to be frequently compared for equality, then it could provide better performance to store their intern values, and perform fast "==" identity tests rather than slower value-based *equals* tests. Be warned however that the *String.intern* method is relatively expensive (even though it is optimized with a native implementation). The operation must search a hashed collection, and possibly add an element to it; plus the collection might have to grow more buckets at regular intervals. Therefore, the overhead of an initialization phase with many *intern* calls must not wipe out the gains of using fast "==" instead of slower *equals*.

```
// FASTER, if intern overhead is eventually offset

public static final String CODE1 = "abc...".intern();
public static final String CODE2 = "efg...".intern();
// ...
public static final String CODEN = "xyz...".intern();

// assume we know 'code' is one of the interned constants
```

```
public void foo( String code )
{
  if ( CODE7 == code )
    // ...
  else
  if ( CODE11 == code )
    // ...
}


// SLOWER

public static final String CODE1 = "abc...";
public static final String CODE2 = "efg...";
  // ...
public static final String CODEN = "xyz...";


public void foo( String code )
{
  if ( CODE7.equals( code ) )
    // ...
  else
  if ( CODE11.equals( code ) )
    // ...
}
```

DECLARE READ-ONLY LOCAL OBJECTS IN STATIC VARIABLES

The following literal array expression

```
  // SLOWER

public void foo()
{
  int[] numbers = { 1, 2, 3 };

    // ...

  ... numbers[ i ] ...
}
```

is, not surprisingly, compiled as though it were written:

```
public void foo()
{
  int[] numbers = new int[ 3 ];
  numbers[ 0 ] = 1;
  numbers[ 1 ] = 2;
  numbers[ 2 ] = 3;
  // ...
}
```

If this is a read-only object and declared as a local variable in a frequently used method, it is not efficient; there is repeated, unnecessary object creation, and several operations required to achieve initialization (which of course gets worse for larger literal arrays).

The solution is to store read-only objects, such as read-only literal arrays, in static variables:

```
// FASTER

private static int[] numbers = { 1, 2, 3 };

  // ...

public void foo()
{
  // ...

  ... numbers[ i ] ...
}
```

A variation on this is that the object may not be read-only, but could be reinitialized:

```
// FASTER

private static HelperObject helper = new HelperObject();

// ...

public void foo()
{
  helper.initialize();

  // ...
}
```

Use Notify When Only One Thread Should Awaken

Object.notifyAll wakes up all threads waiting on an object's monitor. If the design really only requires one thread to wake up when a condition is satisfied, use *notify* to avoid the quite slow and unnecessary work of waking many threads (which are simply going to return to sleep).

On the other hand, we need to be mindful of the implications of limiting notification to *notify*. If many threads are waiting on a condition which is now true, avoiding *notifyAll* will reduce concurrency, and perhaps even cause temporary thread starvation. The concurrency idioms chapter explores this in greater detail.

REPLACE SOME TESTS WITH EXCEPTION HANDLING

The knowledge that an operation is frequently invoked but rarely fails can be exploited to replace the cost of a rarely failing test, such as *instanceof* or *null* tests, with exception handling, and thereby slightly improve performance.

```
  // FASTER (if frequently called)

try
{
  if ( foo.isHappy() )
  {
    // ...
  }
}
catch( NullPointerException ex ) {}


  // SLOWER

if ( foo != null && foo.isHappy() )
{
  // ...
}



  // FASTER (if frequently called)

public void foo( Object o )
{
  // ...
  try
  {
    ((Person)o).bar();
  }
  catch( ClassCastException ex ) {}

  // ...
}


// SLOWER

public void foo( Object o )
{
  // ...

  if ( o instanceof Person )
```

```
{
    ((Person)o).bar();
}

// ...
}
```

USE BITSETS TO REDUCE BOOLEAN STORAGE

If you've really got to squeeze those bits…

It is possible that a representation could require many boolean values (perhaps statistical survey data). Fact: Each boolean variable is represented by a 32-bit value, which is of course not space efficient. Enter the *java.util.BitSet* class. It internally uses a *long* array (each *long* is 64-bits) of at least one element, and provides shifting and logical operators in order to set and manipulate individual bits. Thus, in a tiny *BitSet* object with an array of just one *long* element, 64 boolean states can be represented. On the other hand, *BitSet* operations are slower than setting regular boolean variables.

4 LIBRARY IDIOMS— INTRODUCTION

The *Library Idiom* chapters present an introduction to idioms and best practices of experienced Java developers that emphasize *library* aspects of Java, as opposed to idioms related to the Java language itself. This includes practices related to usage of JDK classes, subtleties in concurrency, and rules for classes overriding *Object* methods that are not obvious at introduction.

Again, our decision about what is "not obvious" is based on our experience interviewing, teaching, and developing with Java. Here are some contrasting examples of what is and is not in the chapter:

Usage relatively obvious from the API docs:

- *Object.equals* can be overridden to provide polymorphic value-based equality checks.

- *java.lang.Constructor* objects are retrieved from *Class.getConstructor*.

Idiomatic usage not self-evident from definition or introductory example:

- Polymorphic *equals* implementations should use *getClass* instead of *instanceof* to maintain symmetry.

- *java.lang.Constructor* objects can be used as factories.

5 LIBRARY IDIOMS— JAVA.LANG.OBJECT

In this chapter

■ Idioms of overriding *equals*, *hashCode*, and other *Object* methods.

---

java.lang.Object is the mother of all Java classes. As such, you might expect that many idioms have emerged from its usage. You would be right. The methods of *Object* are inherited by each class. While some of the methods of *Object* are final, the following are not: *clone, equals, finalize, hashCode, toString*. The author of a class is responsible for guaranteeing that the implementations of these methods are semantically correct.

5.1   THE EQUALS METHOD

The default implementation of *equals* is to check for identity. From the source for *java.lang.Object*:

```
public boolean equals( Object obj )
{
  return this == obj;
}
```

This implementation is adequate for some uses, and is the only reasonable default implementation the JDK could have. But many times, two objects can be equal even though they are distinct. For example, two instances of *Employee* that have the same employee ID must refer to the same person; they should therefore be equal. In such cases, we have to override *Object.equals* to check for **value-based equality**. That is, we need to verify that the two distinct objects have the same values for their fields.

Before we set out to implement *equals*, let's make sure we're all in agreement as to what method we are implementing. The single most important thing to notice about this method is its signature:

```
// parameter is of type Object
public boolean equals( Object object );
```

Many beginning Java programmers mistakenly implement the *equals* method to take a parameter that is of the same type as the receiver:

```
// ERROR: assume receiver is of type Connection
public boolean equals( Connection other );
```

This form does not work. Remember, the signature of a method is determined by the name of the method and the types of its parameters. *equals(Connection)* does not override *equals(Object)* because the two methods have different signatures. This is not an academic distinction. Consider the following simplified class:

```
public class IntHolder
{
  private int value;

  public IntHolder( int value )
  {
    this.value = value;
  }

  public boolean equals( IntHolder other )
  {
    return value == other.value;
  }
}
```

Now consider the following usage of the class:

```
List list = new ArrayList();
list.add( new IntHolder( 5 ) );

  // found is false!

boolean found = list.contains( new IntHolder( 5 ) );
```

We have implemented *ListHolder* to perform a value-based equality check because we want *found* to be *true*. As the list iterates through its collection of objects, it invokes *equals* to determine if the parameter is equal to the objects it contains, so we should be OK. However, because we created our *equals* method to accept instances of *IntHolder*, our *equals* method will never be called by the list. Even though the parameter to the *contains* method was of type *IntHolder*, the signature of the contains method is:

```
public boolean contains( Object object );
```

So by the time the parameter makes it into the *contains* method, the list only knows that it is of type *Object*. The result is that as the list passes it as a parameter in *equals* methods, the rules of method lookup guarantee that *equals(Object)* will be invoked. The moral is that we

always implement *equals(Object)*. Do not implement *equals(<Derived Type>)*.

> Always implement the equals method to accept a parameter of type *Object*.

Now that we know what method we are implementing, we have to determine how to implement it. This process turns out to be surprisingly tricky. There are several steps that need to be followed to implement *equals* in a consistent and efficient manner. It becomes especially tricky since superclass equality needs to be taken into consideration. We divide the canonical *equals* method up into two cases:

- classes that extend *java.lang.Object* directly—for the purposes of this discussion, let's call these classes **base classes**.

- classes that extend *java.lang.Object* indirectly—for the purposes of this discussion, let's call these classes **derived classes**.

We suggest the following canonical form for *equals* in base classes:

Listing 5.1 Base class equals method.

```
// assume Connection extends Object

public boolean equals( Object object )
{
❶   if ( this == object )
        return true;
❷   else if ( object == null || getClass() != object.getClass() )
        return false;

❸   Connection other = (Connection) object;
    return getConnectionId().equals( other.getConnectionId() );
}
```

Let's take each step in turn. Step ❶ is our high-performance short-circuit. The *equals* method could be invoked with the receiver itself as the parameter so it's worth performing this quick check to avoid the gymnastics in the rest of the method.

Step ❷, after ensuring the parameter is not *null,* verifies that these objects are actually of the same class. If they are not, there is no use in proceeding with the tests, the objects can't possibly be equal. Traditionally, developers used the *instanceof* operator for this test. However, as Java frameworks were developed and inheritance was put to work, a fatal flaw was discovered: The *instanceof* operator does not preserve **symmetry** of equality! Recall that symmetry means that if *A=B,* then *B=A.* With *instanceof,* you can have *A.equals(B),* but *!B.equals(A).* This happens when *B*-class extends *A*-class, for while it is true that *B instanceof A*-class, it is not true that *A instanceof B*-class. This is easily remedied by substituting the (almost equally fast) class equality test for the *instanceof* check.

If we have made it to step ❸, then it is time to get down to the business of checking value-equality. Because we passed step ❷, we know we can cast to the type of the receiver and perform our value-equality checks.

For variable names, we use *object* and *other* in all boilerplate checks. We use *object* when the type is still only known to be *Object,* and *other* after the object is known to be another instance of the receiver's type. The names are short and consistent, and because they do not encode the receiver type, they are applicable to any *equals* method. This makes it possible to define hot-key macros for the generic tests.[1]

---

1. Given the frequency with which *equals* needs to be implemented, and the subtlety of the code, we highly recommend creating macros for this boilerplate code. Assign a hot-key to each macro for maximum convenience.

For derived classes, we recommend the following form:

Listing 5.2 Derived class equals method.

```
    // assume OneWayConnection extends Connection

    public boolean equals( Object object )
    {
❶   if ( this == object )
        return true;
❷   else if ( !super.equals( object ) )
        return false;

❸   OneWayConnection other = (OneWayConnection) object;
        return getDirection().equals( other.getDirection() );
    }
```

Step ❶ is our friend the short-circuit. We reproduce the check here to take full advantage of it, otherwise some of its high performance characteristic is lost with the base class delegation.

Step ❷ is where the derived class boilerplate check differs from the base class boiler-plate check. Instead of performing a class equality check, we delegate to the base class implementation. The base class implementation is responsible for the class-equality-check and the value-checks on the base class data. The class-equality-check need not be duplicated in the derived class. It is executed a single time in the base class. This is enough to ensure that we can cast it to the appropriate type in each derived class. The base class value-checks will be performed in the base class implementation to ensure maximum information-hiding. This prevents the derived class from being tightly coupled to the base class. If the objects are deemed equal by the base class implementation, then the derived class value-checks will be performed after the *equals* method unwinds from the *super.equals* invocations. Otherwise, the objects are not equal, so return *false*.

By step ❸, we know the two objects have the same class. Therefore, we can cast directly to the receiver's type and perform the derived class checks.

Implementing *equals* like this is a bit of a chore, but with macros and short-cut keys, at least the typing effort is eliminated. In return, we get a very robust implementa-tion of *equals*—one that is well suited to complex frameworks. There is one *caveat*: If the design is in flux and classes are moved up and down the class hierarchy, the *equals* methods must be kept in sync. That is, if a base class becomes a derived class or *vice versa*, make sure the *equals* method boilerplate is changed as well.

There is another very important thing to remember when implementing *equals*: the *equals-hashCode* contract:

> The *equals-hashCode* contract states that two objects that are equal must return the same *hashCode*.

What this means is that because we have now implemented *equals* to perform a value-based equality check, we must now implement *hashCode* to return the same value for equal objects. This is critical because our objects may (now or in the future) be used as keys in a hashing container. Let's go back to the *IntHolder* example and consider its use as a key for a hash map:

```
Map map = new HashMap();
map.put( new IntHolder( 5 ), new Object() );

    // value == null !!!

Object value = map.get( new IntHolder( 5 ) );
```

We got a very unexpected result because we did not implement *hashCode* to be consistent with our *equals* method; we broke the *equals-hashCode* contract. To prevent these results, we have to implement *hashCode*. See below.

5.2 THE HASHCODE METHOD

hashCode is invoked by hashing containers as a means to retrieve an array index from an object for fast lookup. To help us understand the role of hashing, let's consider the case of the *HashMap.get* operation.

Internally, the *HashMap* class is implemented as an array of linked lists (called **hash buckets**). Each link in a list contains a key-value pair (stored into the hash map with the *put* operation). For a given index in the array, all of the keys in the bucket at that index have the same hash code modulo the size of the array.

A *HashMap.get* operation takes the key parameter, invokes the *hashCode* method on it, reduces this to a number less than the size of the array using modular arithmetic, looks up the buckets at this index, and iterates through the bucket invoking *equals* on each key to determine which key is equal to the provided parameter. Once found, the value associated with that key is returned.

So, where a list will iterate through all of its elements (invoking *equals* on each one) to find an object's position in the array, a hashing container uses the hash code of the object to (often drastically) reduce the number of *equals* comparisons that need to be made. The hash code of the key parameter provides a first guess as to where to find the value. The *equals* invocations focus that guess down to the answer. This process can be extremely fast, and is the reason that hashing containers are so valuable for high performance associative lookup.

There are several important things to learn from this:

1. Objects that are equal must generate the same hash code. This guarantees that two equal objects will be placed in the same bucket. If equal objects do not return the same hash code, they will wind up in different buckets and the lookup will always fail.

2. Objects that are not equal should ideally generate different hash codes. In fact, the generated hash codes should create an even distribution of objects over the

hash collection's buckets. This will minimize collisions (that is, the buckets in the hash map's collection of entries will be about the same size), and will therefore minimize the number of times the hashing collection has to invoke the *equals* method on our key.

3. The value of the hash code of a key stored in the hash map should not change while the key is stored in the hash map. This would yield unpredictable results for the hash maps' methods. Unless the hash map is rehashed, the key will be stuck in the wrong bucket; its neighbors will all have a different hash code.

4. If anything changes within the object that would result in a change in the value of the *equals* method, then the value returned by the *hashCode* method must be changed to keep in sync. This ensures that equal objects have equal hash codes. Note that if the object is a key in a hashing container, the container should be rehashed. However, it is not always convenient or possible to do this. This is a common gotcha with basing *hashCode* on mutable data, and there is no easy way around it.

5. The *hashCode* method should ideally be fast to invoke. It is supposed to be a fast first guess. Cache the value of the hash code within the object if it's immutable or if extreme hashing performance is needed. This prevents the need to recompute the value every time the *hashCode* method is invoked. See the chapter on high-performance hashing to see *String* versus a hash code-caching *Key* class. The *Key* class is twice as fast!

To fix the *IntHolder* example from the *equals* section to return hash codes consistent with the way *IntHolder.equals* is defined, we add the following *hashCode* method:

```
/**
 * Note that this implementation meets the requirement that all
 * IntHolder's that are equal return the same value. If the
 * IntHolder's represent an even distribution, then so will
 * the hash codes.
 */
public int hashCode()
{
  return value;
}
```

Not all cases are as easy as the *IntHolder* class. Many classes have several fields that are used to determine equality. A general rule of thumb is that a reasonable hash code can be formed by adding the hash code of each field (assuming the underlying hash codes are evenly distributed [Uzgalis 1991]).

```
/**
 * An Employee object may have a hash code like this one
 */
public int hashCode()
{
  return firstName.hashCode() + lastName.hashCode();
}
```

If this process results in a poor distribution, consider moving to a more advanced hash algorithm.

5.3   THE CLONE METHOD

Every object has a *clone* method—it inherits the implementation in class *Object*—but not every object can be cloned. The reason is that the default implementation of *clone* is to throw an exception unless the receiver implements the *Cloneable* interface. (Note also that *Object.clone* is a protected method and thus inaccessible to most callers.) If the object implements *Cloneable*, the *clone* operation will succeed. The implementers of Java chose to implement *clone* in this way because it gives the developer the power to decide if the default implementation of *clone* is adequate, yet it still allows a default implementation to be available to all objects.

Note that this is an example of the *marker interface* idiom. By implementing *Cloneable*, the author declares that cloning is allowed without actually having to implement any methods.

Sometimes, however, the default implementation may not be adequate. Consider that a clone operation returns a copy of the receiver. Should the copy be a *shallow* copy or a *deep* copy? That is, should only the receiver be copied, or should the entire object graph of the receiver be copied? Maybe a "partial" deep-copy should be performed. It all depends upon the context.

The implementation in *Object* is to return a shallow copy. Subclasses can utilize this method by merely implementing *Cloneable*. Alternatively, as a convenience to client objects, the default implementation can be overridden and the *CloneNotSupportedException* can be caught:

```
    // shallow copy clone
public Object clone()
{
  try
  {
    return super.clone();
  }
  catch( CloneNotSupportedException ex )
  {
    return null; // can't happen
  }
}
```

If a deep copy is needed, the *Object* version of clone is used to create the initial shallow copy, and the object fields are set separately. For example:

```
    // deep copy clone
/**
 * Note that we catch CloneNotSupportedException as
 * a convenience to clients. We could alternatively
 * throw a RuntimeException.
 */
public Object clone()
{
  try
  {
    Employee other = (Employee) super.clone();
    other.setBenefits( getBenefits().clone() );
    return other;
```

```
    }
    catch( CloneNotSupportedException ex )
    {
      return null;
    }
  }
```

The *CloneNotSupportedException* is caught as a convenience to clients. Clients programming directly to the interface of the class—as opposed to the interface presented in *Object*—will therefore not have to catch this exception. In theory, the *CloneNotSupportedException* could be used by a class to indicate an error in cloning. If you decide to use this approach, do not catch the exception, re-declare it in the *throws* clause.

5.4   THE FINALIZE METHOD

The *finalize* method is invoked by the garbage collector to ensure that the garbage object has a chance to perform the necessary cleanup before its destruction. This is particularly important when the object holds onto expensive resources like sockets and files that need to be closed.

Because of the random nature of garbage collection, you can never know exactly when the *finalize* method will be invoked. For this reason, do not rely on *finalize* methods as the only way to free up expensive resources. The garbage collector may take considerable time to garbage collect the object. In fact, for many platforms, the existence of a custom *finalize* method may make it take longer for the object to get garbage collected. What's more, finalizers may not be run on system exit (see *System.runFinalizersOnExit*) and in general there is no way to guarantee they will be executed.

The general rule is that expensive resources should be freed up explicitly when they are no longer needed. For many resources (threads, files, sockets, and so on) it will usually be completely obvious when they can be released or closed. The *finalize* method, on the other hand, should be used as a last-ditch cleanup effort and for de-registration.

> Do not rely on the *finalize* method to free up expensive resources. These should be freed manually. Use *finalize* for de-registration and/or last-ditch cleanup.

Implementing the *finalize* method is very simple, once you know the correct form. Let's get straight to that form:

```
   public void finalize()
   {
❶    try
     {
       // custom finalize logic
     }
     finally
     {
❷      super.finalize();
     }
   }
```

Step ❶ is used to perform cleanup necessary for this object. Though any exception can be thrown from *finalize*, the exception is ignored. Because a thrown exception would prevent us from completing step ❷, we wrap all custom cleanup in a try-finally.

Step ❷ ensures that the superclass version of finalize is invoked. The superclass version must be invoked because our *finalize* method overrides the superclass version, and we may therefore be preventing it from cleaning up resources internal to the superclass implementation. Note that the superclass version must be invoked as the last step to prevent cleanup in the superclass from invalidating the object before we get a chance to cleanup. In general, the subclass may make assumptions about the behavior in the superclass—behavior that undoubtedly changes after finalization.

The superclass, however, does not care about what goes on in the subclass. The situation is analogous to what happens in constructors. For example:

```
public Manager( String id, String name, Collection minions )
{
   super( id, name );
   this.minions = minions;
}
```

The subclass initializes at the superclass level first. Conversely, we want to de-initialize at the subclass level first. Note that the compiler ensures that the constructor chaining happens from the top down, but does *not* ensure that finalizer chaining happens from the bottom up.

5.5   THE TOSTRING METHOD

toString is the simplest of all the methods of *Object* we have to implement. Generate the string so that it provides a descriptive, human-readable form of the object. *toString* is invoked when the object is printed to the console or in a GUI, and implicitly when concatenated to a string with +. If this printing is occurring frequently, and the nature of the string is relatively complex, consider caching the value.

```
public String toString()
{
   if ( toString == null )
     toString = // ...

   return toString;
}
```

Be careful here. If the data that forms the string version of the object changes, the string will need to be recomputed.

6 LIBRARY IDIOMS— REFLECTION

In this chapter

- Idioms using the classes in the java.lang.reflect package, and the java.beans.BeanInfo class.

Reflection is one of the most powerful features of the Java language. It is certainly one of the coolest. Reflective programming, also called meta-programming (and related to meta-data or data-driven designs), allows for radical new designs and implementations. Some of these are terminally clever, some of them border on the bizarre. And therein lies the problem with reflection. It's one of those "enough rope" situations—you've been given the rope, do you build a bridge or hang yourself?

Too often, reflection is abused. One of our colleagues is fond of asking interview candidates if they know reflection. If they answer yes, he then asks them why? The implication is that there are few cases when reflection is desirable, and even fewer where it is required. We have certainly seen our share of abuses of reflection.

The techniques presented here hit the sweet spot for most application developers. While some specialized developers (for example, those building ORBs, O-R mapping frameworks, or AI systems) will want to master the full complexity of reflection, most of us should stick to the techniques presented here. They are battle-proven uses of reflection that can significantly improve a design.

6.1 DYNAMIC CLASSLOADING

One of Java's most powerful features is dynamic classloading. Dynamic classloading was one of the primary contributors to the explosive rate at which Java became *the* Internet programming language. Indeed, without dynamic classloading, applets would not have been possible.

Dynamic classloading is often used for custom class loading. In the case of applets, the source is a web server. In other cases, the source may be a database, a JNDI directory, or an encrypted file. Classloading can also be used in its most dynamic form: on-the-fly code generation. In this scenario, bytecode is generated on-the-fly and linked directly into the VM. In each of these scenarios, a custom classloader will need to be created.

Beyond custom class sources, there are important uses of dynamic classloading that do not involve implementing a custom classloader. One of the most important uses is for dynamic service registration. Many applications are organized into pluggable services. The application must be decoupled from the specific services, and yet it must somehow force the services to register. The Java mechanism for solving this problem involves three important Java features: system properties, dynamic classloading, and *static* blocks.

Consider the following code:

```
String service = System.getProperty( "com.foo.service", DEFAULT_SERVICE );
Class.forName( service ); // link in the class
```

```
// this is the loaded class

public class SecurityService
{

  static
  {
    SystemController.registerService( new SecurityService() );
  }

  // ...
```

Here a system property is accessed to determine the correct service. The query is provided a suitable default, in case no special service has been set. Once found, the service class is linked into the VM with the *Class.forName* operation. This operation in turn invokes the *static* block of the service class—in this case *SecurityService*, which then can perform the necessary registration or initialization. (For brevity, the error handling is not shown; *ClassNotFoundException* should be dealt with.)

A similar approach involves external instantiation of the service:

```
String name = System.getProperty( "com.foo.service", DEFAULT_SERVICE );
Class serviceClass = Class.forName( name );
IService service= (IService) serviceClass.newInstance();
```

In this version, the class is instantiated directly and is cast to the appropriate interface. This version gives the control to the class that is loading the service, but also increases coupling. (For instance, the controller is now dependent upon the existence of an accessible default constructor.)

With either approach, the correct service class name can be set in the system properties from a properties file, the command line, or from within another part of the application (for example, a user-specified field in a GUI). The following demonstrates setting the property from the command line:

```
>java -Dcom.foo.service=com.foo.SecureProvider com.foo.Main
```

A commonly encountered deficiency with this mechanism is that each system property must have a unique name. So, for instance, there cannot be two properties with the name *"com.foo.service,"* even if the application is designed to load multiple services. This is commonly circumvented by packing multiple values into the same property using some kind of delimiter character. The JDBC API uses this approach for driver registration. The *DriverManager* class looks at the *jdbc.drivers* property (the value of which is expected to be a colon-delimited list of driver classes) and iteratively links in each specified class. We can use this approach to load :

```
String services = System.getProperty( "com.foo.service" );

    // tokenize on SEPARATOR, which could be the colon character

StringTokenizer tokens = new StringTokenizer( services, SEPARATOR );

while( tokens.hasMoreTokens() )
{
  try { Class.forName( tokens.nextToken() ); }
  catch( ClassNotFoundException ex )
  {
    // ...
  }
}
```

There is an alternative to using a single property for multiple values: mangle the property name for each value, and use *String.startsWith*, instead of the implicit *String.equals*, to detect the key value. Take the following example:

```
Properties env = System.getProperties();

for ( Iterator i = env.keySet().iterator(); i.hasNext(); )
{
  String key = (String) i.next();

  if ( key.startsWith( SERVICE_PROPERTY ) )
  {
    try
    {
      Class.forName( env.getProperty( key ) );
    }
```

```
    catch( ClassNotFoundException ex )
    {
      // ...
    }
  }
}
```

In this code, the system properties are iterated through to find property names that begin with the string *SERVICE_PROPERTY*. The application can be started from a properties file like the following:

```
# This properties file is loaded by the SystemController. It
# initializes services which are indicated with keys that begin
# with "com.foo.service".

# note that these are just strings, not arrary element
# assignments!

com.foo.service[1]=com.foo.security.SecurityService
com.foo.service[2]=com.foo.transaction.TransactionService
com.foo.service[3]=com.foo.concurrency.ConcurrencyService
```

Though ignored here, the numbers could even be used to create an ordering, to index into a list, or for some other custom parameterization.

6.2 Method Objects for Pluggable Behavior

Pluggable Behavior [Beck 1997] is a popular pattern to parameterize the behavior of an object. In the *Pluggable Method* variation, *java.lang.reflect.Method* objects are used to parameterize behavior[1].

This approach is most often used with metadata-based designs; that is, when there are "data about data" representations that drive some kind of logic. Examples include object-relational mapping systems that can translate between object-oriented and relational schemas, and inference engines that reason with knowledge representation structures such as rules, frames, and so on—techniques originating from the discipline of Artificial Intelligence.

We will examine a fragment of an object-relational mapping system to see how metadata and *Pluggable Method* can by applied. In this example the key idea is that *ColumnBeanPropertySchemaMapping* objects are parameterized with a *Pluggable Method* so that this one class can be conveniently used to invoke *any* setter method on *any* class of object.

ColumnBeanPropertySchemaMapping objects are created to represent the mapping between a particular column in some table, and a particular JavaBeans property of an object. Note that the property name ("salary" in this case) is passed in as a string. This will be used to find the read and write methods associated with the property name.

```
// Construct with the Column, Bean class, and Bean property name.

ColumnBeanPropertySchemaMapping mapping =
   new ColumnBeanPropertySchemaMapping( column, beanClass, "salary" );
```

---

1. An implementation of *Pluggable Behavior* that uses anonymous inner classes is covered in the language idioms chapter.

Later, when a *java.sql.ResultSet* is generated via a JDBC call, this mapping object can be used to extract a value from the *ResultSet* and insert it into the object.

```
mapping.mapFromResultSetToObject( resultSet, object );
```

In the definition of the mapping class, it remembers the *Column* and the *java.lang.reflect.Method*s to use in the mapping.

```
public final class ColumnBeanPropertySchemaMapping
{
  private Method writeMethod;
  private Method readMethod;
  private Column column;
  // ...
```

The constructor uses *java.beans.Introspector* and helper methods to find the *Method* objects.

```
public ColumnBeanPropertySchemaMapping
  ( Column column, Class beanClass, String propName )
  throws MetadataException, IntrospectionException
{
  this.column = column;

  BeanInfo info = Introspector.getBeanInfo( beanClass );
  this.writeMethod = getWriteMethodFor( info, propName );
  this.readMethod = getReadMethodFor( info, propName );
}
```

The *getWriteMethodFor* helper method below finds the *PropertyDescriptor* for the object; statement ❷ contains the critical step of finding the actual method to be used.

As an aside, note that a *java.beans.BeanInfo* object and its associated *Descriptors* contain a wealth of useful reflection-level information that can be used to help with metadata and reflective-programming designs.

Observe that at the test at ❶ there is the chance for failure. For example, the property name, which is being passed in as a string, may be spelled incorrectly. This exemplifies a key disadvantage of *Pluggable Method* designs: They can fail at runtime because of mapping errors that the compiler cannot spot, usually due to information being stored in strings that is ultimately used to try and find *Method* objects.

```
private Method getWriteMethodFor( BeanInfo info, String propName )
  throws MetadataException, IntrospectionException
{
  PropertyDescriptor[] descriptors = info.getPropertyDescriptors();

  // search for a descriptor matching propName

  for( int i = 0; i < descriptors.length; i++ )
  {
❶   if ( descriptors[ i ].getName().equals( propName ) )
❷     return descriptors[ i ].getWriteMethod();
  }

  throw new MetadataException( "Property method missing: " + propName );
}
```

Finally, in the next listing the *mapFromResultSetToObject* method illustrates exercising a pluggable method in Java, using the *Method.invoke* operation at ❶, which invokes the *Method* on a receiver object passed as a parameter, and with the parameters to the method (wrapped in an array) as the second parameter.

A language feature similar to *Method.invoke* is the key ingredient in any object-oriented programming language in order to make *Pluggable Method* designs possible.

```
public void mapFromResultSetToObject( ResultSet set, Object object )
{
  try
  {
    Object columnVal = set.getObject( column.getName() );
❶   writeMethod.invoke( object, new Object[] { columnVal } );
  }
  catch( InvocationTargetException ex )
  {
    // ...
  }
}
```

To reiterate, the main defect with *Pluggable Method* is that it is not as type-safe as *Pluggable Behavior Object* (using anonymous inner classes, described later); runtime errors can arise during the mapping of a string indicating a method name to a *Method*.

Surprisingly (to some), benchmarks reveal that *Method.invoke* is *not* much slower than regular method invocation.[1] Furthermore, the usual contexts of its use—such as metadata mapping—are such that the invocations of *Method.invoke* do not usually happen in high-frequency performance-critical sections. Of course, if performance does become a problem, profiling will reveal if *Method.invoke* is to blame, or if the cause is elsewhere—which it usually will be.

6.3 CONSTRUCTOR OBJECTS AS FACTORIES

Interfaces are used to decouple clients from implementations. However, because interfaces can only declare methods, and not constructors, they do not provide any means of decoupling a client from the *construction* of an implementation. The *Factory* pattern [GHJV 1995] allows a client to be independent of the way in which implementations are instantiated. It usually involves some other class, a factory, that can be used to create the implementation. The factory is dependent upon the implementation class, the client is coupled only to the interface.

In some systems, the factory pattern can become quite complex, often involving hierarchies of factories, factory interfaces, and so forth. On the other hand, Java provides a very lightweight factory mechanism in the form of *java.lang.reflect.Constructor*. Instances of class *Constructor*, obtained from *Class.getConstructor*, represent actual constructors defined in a class. Once a constructor is obtained, it can be

---

1. Excluding inlined methods.

invoked by passing the appropriate arguments (in the form of an array of *Object*) to the *Constructor.newInstance* method.

The following code demonstrates using a *Constructor* object as a factory for *Collection* objects:

```
private Constructor factory;

public void setFactory( Constructor factory )
{
   this.factory = factory;
}

private Collection createCollection()
{
   try
   {
     return (Collection) factory.newInstance( new Object[ 0 ] );
   }
   catch( Exception ex )
   {
     throw new RuntimeException( ex.toString() ); // for example only
   }
}
```

The class in which this code is declared thus has a means of obtaining new collections in a way that is independent of the specific collection class. Some external entity can specify the appropriate collection constructor. For example, if the system needs to use *ArrayList* objects, this could be achieved with the following code:

```
object.setFactory( ArrayList.class.getConstructor( new Class[ 0 ] );
```

This version of the Factory pattern is extremely lightweight in that it involves no custom factory classes or interfaces. Note also that the *setFactory* method could check the declaring class to ensure the objects it constructs are of the correct type. This provides a certain measure of type safety.

The *Dynamic Classloading* idiom is often used to "complete the loop" for this idiom. For example, the class from which the *Constructor* is obtained can be set as a system property and loaded through the *Class.forName* method. Alternatively, another module can load the class, and the dynamically loaded class can invoke the *setFac-*

tory method from within its static block. See the dynamic classloading section for more on these approaches.

6.4 INTROSPECTOR AND BEANINFO FOR REFLECTIVE PROGRAMMING

Within the *java.beans* package is the *Introspector* class, which can be used to obtain reflective information about any Java class. It is a higher-level alternative to the *java.lang.reflect* package, which contains the primitive operations to obtain reflective information. When applied to any class (not just an intended "JavaBean" class), the *Introspector* returns an instance of a class that implements the *BeanInfo* interface. This object contains reflective information describing the public features (public getter and setter methods, action methods, and event support) of the class that was analyzed. For example:

```
BeanInfo info = Introspector.getBeanInfo( employee.getClass() );
```

Although it was originally designed for use by IDE-vendor programmers in support of their creation of JavaBeans visual programming tools, the *BeanInfo* object is also of use to designers of reflective or metadata-based designs.

The advantage of using the *BeanInfo* object is that it separates the notion of *logical* features (properties, action methods, and events) from their physical implementation with methods and fields. This is achievable by creating a special *BeanInfo* class to accompany the bean class. For example, for the class *Employee*, if one creates the class *EmployeeBeanInfo*, then the *Introspector* will find it (by the naming convention) and use it to create an instance of a *BeanInfo*. The object contains many elements, such as a set of *PropertyDescriptor* instances that describe the logical properties of an

Employee, such as "name," "hireDate," and so on. A *PropertyDescriptor* describes the type of the property, and its getter and setter methods, among other qualities. For example:

```
BeanInfo info = Introspector.getBeanInfo( employee.getClass() );
PropertyDescriptor[] descriptors = info.getPropertyDescriptors();
Method getter = descriptors[0].getReadMethod();
Method setter = descriptors[0].getWriteMethod();
Class type = descriptors[0].getPropertyType();
```

The read and write methods are associated with a logical property—an abstraction. This allows the designer to change the underlying information associated with a property, without changing the property name. For example, originally the read and write methods associated with the logical property "hireDate" might be *getHireDate* and *setHireDate*. However, the methods could be changed to *getStartDate* and *setStartDate* without changing the name of the property—it can remain "hireDate." This increases the flexibility of metadata-based designs, which can be coupled to logical properties, rather than to underlying methods and fields. If the developer only uses *java.lang.reflect*, their designs must be coupled to the underlying physical implementation of a class; the *BeanInfo* object adds a layer of logical abstraction and thus lowers the coupling to implementations.

7 LIBRARY IDIOMS— CONCURRENCY

In this chapter

- Best practices when writing a multi-threaded application.

This chapter not only describes common Java concurrency idioms, it also goes into more detail than usual on the nature of Java concurrency. Concurrency is one of the few complex Java topics, and it is rife with gotchas and pitfalls. Some of the more common ones are dealt with here.

See [Lea 1996] by Doug Lea, one of the foremost luminaries on the subject of Java concurrency, for a comprehensive treatment of multi-threaded Java programming.

7.1 NON-ATOMIC CHECK-AND-ACT CAUSES MOST RACE-CONDITIONS

Check-and-act code follows the following template:

```
if ( condition )
   performAction();
```

The majority of race-conditions involve non-atomic check-and-act sequences. The typical scenario goes:

1. thread *A* checks *condition* and *condition* is *true*

2. thread scheduler schedules thread *B* to run

3. thread *B* performs a sequence of actions that causes *condition* to become *false*

4. thread scheduler schedules *A* to run

5. thread *A* executes *performAction* under the assumption that condition is still *true*

Check-and-act sequences must be atomic so that the action can in fact proceed with assurance that the condition is true. Sometimes, check-and-act sequences are much more difficult to spot than this. Consider:

```
public String getBarString()
{
   checkBar();
   return bar.toString();
}

public synchronized void checkBar()
{
   if ( bar == null )
     throw new IllegalArgumentException( "Bar is null" );
}
```

Though the check-and-act seems to include only *checkBar*, it actually includes *get-BarString*. Unless *getBarString* is synchronized, the value of bar may become null between the *checkBar* invocation and the *bar.toString* invocation.

Moral: Look very closely at all code to find all check-and-act sequences.

7.2 NON-ATOMIC TREATMENT OF DOUBLE AND LONG

There are two types in Java that are comprised of eight bytes: *long* and *double*. Because a word in Java is four bytes, *long* and *double* are the only two types comprised of two words, and they are the only types for which a main memory read or write is not atomic [GJS 1996]. In fact, a read or write of one of these types may— and in general, does—occur as two 32-bit operations. This means that the following code is not thread-safe:

```
public long getAgeOfUniverse()
{
   return ageOfUniverse;
}
```

The problem is that the read of the *ageOfUniverse* variable can occur half-way before a write, and halfway after a write. The value returned is comprised of the first word of the original value, and the second word of the updated value. In effect, the value returned is neither the value before the write or the value after the write—it is a combination of the two!

To prevent this, synchronize all access to *long* and *double* fields. (Alternatively, one could declare the fields *volatile*. This works because one of the rules of *volatile* fields is that all writes and reads to and from main memory be atomic. Frankly, use of *volatile* is extremely rare and a design that relied upon it for thread safety would be very subtle. Stick with synchronization if possible.)

7.3 NON-ATOMIC TREATMENT OF INCREMENT/DECREMENT

The ++ and -- operations are not atomic. They represent a read and a write—two operations, not one.

```
// not thread-safe!

public int getNextCount()
{
  return count++;
}
```

Make sure this action is synchronized against all other reads and write of the variable.

7.4 TWEAKING PRIORITY DOES NOT ELIMINATE RACE-CONDITIONS

A common novice mistake when trying to eliminate a race-condition is to tweak thread priorities via *Thread.setPriority*. For instance, if two threads are dead-locking, one way to try to prevent the deadlock is to increase the priority on one thread so that it finishes before the other thread tries to get the lock that causes the deadlock. This reasonable sounding attempt is almost guaranteed *not* to work. What's worse, it may actually help in many cases, and therefore *seem* to be a solution. What it does, however, is make the race-condition less likely to occur, and therefore harder to detect and debug. Because the race-condition occurs less frequently, the tester or developer may assume it is fixed. The application makes it through QA and then deadlocks out in the field.

Do not try to eliminate race-conditions with thread priority tweaks. Thread priorities are only hints to the thread scheduler, they do not guarantee anything. They should be used as high-level indicators of the importance of a thread's task. They are applicable at a time-granularity of hours, minutes, or possibly seconds. They are *not* useful for race-conditions, the time windows of which are measured in milliseconds or microseconds.

7.5   OBJECT.WAIT RELEASES LOCK ON RECEIVER ONLY

The semantics of *Object.wait* are among the trickiest in all of Java. One of its lesser known qualities is that it only releases the lock for the object on which it is invoked. Consider the following code:

```
synchronized ( objectA )
{
  synchronized ( objectB )
  {
    objectB.wait();
  }
}
```

The *wait* invocation on *objectB* releases all synchronization locks acquired by the invoking thread on *objectB*. However, the synchronization lock held for *objectA* is *not* released. This is a common cause of deadlocks.

7.6   NOTIFY IS AN OPTIMIZATION OF NOTIFYALL

It is well known that *notify* chooses a single waiting thread to wake-up, whereas *notifyAll* wakes all waiting threads. The general rule is to always use *notifyAll* to wake threads. Treat *notify* as an optimization of *notifyAll*. Use it only if you determine *notifyAll* to be excessively detrimental to performance.

The reason for this awkward rule is that it is not always clear whether *notify* is waking the right thread. In general, if any thread will do, then *notify* would work fine. It often happens, however, that any old thread will not do. Consider the example in Listing 7.1 adapted from [Lea 1997a]:

Listing 7.1 A BoundedBuffer class.

```
/*
 * Note: Uses array instead of list to achieve maximum
 * performance. This is common in low-level containers,
 * but we still recommend using List over arrays for
 * most application uses.
 */
public class BoundedBuffer
{
  private final int max;
  private Object[] data;
  private int size = 0;
  private int head = 0;
  private int tail = 0;

  public BoundedBuffer( int max )
  {
    this.max = max;
    data = new Object[ max ];
  }

  public synchronized void put( Object object )
  {
    while ( size == max )
      try { wait(); } catch ( InterruptedException ex ) {}

    size++;
    data[ tail ] = object; // store at tail
    tail = ( tail + 1 ) % max;

    if ( size == 1 ) // no longer empty
      notifyAll();
  }

  public synchronized Object get()
  {
    while ( size == 0 )
      try { wait(); } catch (InterruptedException ex ) {}

    Object object = data[ head ]; // remove at head
    size--;
    head = ( head + 1 ) % max;
```

```
    if ( size == max - 1 )
        notifyAll();

    return object;
    }
}
```

The *BoundedBuffer* class represents a data store capable of holding *max* number of objects. In this example, a *put* invocation is blocked if the buffer is full, and a *get* invocation is blocked if the buffer is empty.

Use of *notify* here would result in a subtle race-condition under heavy concurrency. Hold onto your seats, this one is a doozy!

1. The buffer is full.

2. Multiple *put* invocations are blocked waiting for *size* to become less than *max*.

3. A *get* invocation acquires the lock.

4. Multiple *get* invocations arrive and are blocked before entering the method because the other *get* holds the lock.

5. The original *get* removes an item from the buffer and invokes *notify* because the buffer is no longer full.

6. The notified *put* awakens and tries, along with the blocking *get* methods, to acquire the lock.

7. The original *get* finishes invocation and releases the lock.

8. One of the blocked *get* invocations wins the lock (over the other *get* invocations and the notified *put* invocation). It removes an object from the buffer, but as the buffer was not full, does not invoke a *notify*. It then exits and releases the lock.

We are left with a buffer with two empty slots, but only one executing *put* operation! The other *put* operations are still blocked. Instead, the *get* operation should notify all waiting *put* invocations so they may have a chance to fill the buffer. The *while* loop will guarantee that the notified put methods do not overfill the buffer. (See the section on guarded suspension.)

Note that in many cases, *notifyAll* causes unnecessary context switching in those cases when only a single thread should be allowed to proceed. In low-level objects like containers, thread primitives like semaphores, and so forth, this is justification enough to try to optimize out the *notifyAll* and replace with *notify.* For non-systems level classes, however, *notifyAll* will rarely cause significant performance problems.

7.7 FACTS ABOUT JAVA THREAD SCHEDULING

If there were one word that described the nature of Java thread scheduling, it would be *unpredictable*. It is a random business, and attempts to pigeon-hole it into some preconceived notion of order will certainly cause headaches down the road. In particular, remember all of the following important facts about Java thread scheduling [Lea 1997a]:

- Java does not guarantee the highest priority thread will always run (though in practice, this will often be the case for most platforms).

- Threads of equal priority are not necessarily scheduled FIFO.

- Object locks are not necessarily granted FIFO.

- Threads in a wait-set are not necessarily notified FIFO.

- *Thread.yield* may yield control to a thread of lower, equal, or higher priority.

7.8 USE WHILE LOOPS FOR GUARDED SUSPENSION

Some multithreaded designs require one thread to wait until a given condition is met. The technique, called *Guarded Suspension* [Lea 1996], relies upon use of *Object.wait*. Unfortunately, the semantics of *Object.wait* are often misunderstood by those new to Java concurrency. First, you must hold the lock on the receiver before invoking its *wait* method. If not, the *IllegalMonitorStateException* will be thrown. Failure to understand this is usually temporary, as soon as the program is run the developer will be confronted with the exception. The second, and much more subtle misconception involves the behavior of *wait* in relationship to locks. When *wait* is invoked, it *releases all locks held on the receiver*. This seemingly innocuous statement causes all kinds of headache. Consider the following code:

```
public synchronized void foo() throws InterruptedException
{
  partA();
  wait();
  partB();
}
```

The novice programmer might think that this action is atomic because it occurs within a *synchronized* method. In fact, the *wait* invocation releases all locks held on the receiver by the thread. (If it didn't, a *synchronized notify* invocation would deadlock!) The occurrence of *wait* in the body of the *foo* method breaks the atomicity: *foo* effectively becomes two atomic actions. The result is that the *foo* method is conceptually similar to the following code:

```
public void almostFoo() throws InterruptedException
{
  synchronized ( this )
  {
    partA();
  }
```

```
// halt

synchronized ( this )
{
  partB();
}
}
```

This means that once the receiver is notified (via *notify* of *notifyAll*), the invoking thread must contend with other threads for the lock on the object. This exposes the two-phase nature of *wait*. The thread can be waiting to get the lock even after it is notified out of the *wait* method. Messing with your mind yet?

It is important to note that threads emerging from *wait* do not receive any precedence over other threads in terms of re-acquisition of the lock. Failure to recognize this can result in subtle race-conditions. Consider the following:

```
public synchronized void lock() throws InterruptedException
{
  if ( isLocked )
    wait();

  isLocked = true;
}

public synchronized void unLock()
{
  isLocked = false;
  notify();
}
```

Imagine this code is used in the following way. Before performing an action, *lock* is invoked, after performing the action, *unlock* is invoked. The intent of this code is to allow one thread through at any given time. Once a thread has invoked lock, other threads will read *isLocked* as *true* and wait. This code is not thread-safe.

Assume one thread is waiting and that the lock is released by invocation of *unLock*. The waiting thread wakes up out of the wait and proceeds to re-synchronize on the receiver. However, the thread-scheduler decides to allow a third thread to execute, it gets the lock on the object, enters the lock method, detects *isLocked* to be *false*, sets *isLocked* to be *true*, and exits the method. Well our awakening thread is now given processor time and it re-synchronizes on the receiver. It is expecting *isLocked* to be *false*, after all it was just notified by the original locking thread. It sets *isLocked* to be *true* (though it already was) and proceeds. We now have two threads through the locking mechanism. Not a very effective locking mechanism!

Fortunately, this is easily solve by replacing the *if* with a *while*:

```
public synchronized void lock() throws InterruptedException
{
  while ( isLocked )
    wait();

  isLocked = true;
}
```

As a general rule, replace all if-waits with while-waits. In those cases where an if-wait would have sufficed, a while-wait merely adds a second conditional test. Unless the conditional test is computationally expensive, this is an unnoticeable overhead. On the other hand, in those cases where a while-wait is required, an if-wait can result in extremely onerous bugs.

7.9 CLASS SYNCHRONIZATION

Synchronization frequently needs to be applied at the class level. For example, if a *Singleton* is lazily initialized, the initialization code will need to be synchronized at the class level to prevent multiple invocations of the initialization logic. This is easily managed with *synchronized static* methods. The effect is to acquire the lock associated with the class itself, not with a particular instance.

```
// method is synchronized on the Class object for the declaring class

private static synchronized void initializeInstance()
  {
    if ( instance == null )
      instance = new Singleton();
  }
```

Sometimes, it is not convenient to invoke a *synchronized static* method. Synchronized blocks are used on the instance side to avoid having to pass several parameters, or to avoid having to create complex return values:

```
synchronized ( this )
{
  // ...
}
```

The analog on the class side is to synchronize on the *Class* object that represents the declaring class. That is, to acquire the lock for the *Class* object that represents the declaring class. This is achieved by obtaining a reference to the *Class* object via the *Object.getClass* method if the synchronized block is being invoked from within an instance method:

```
// block is synchronized on the Class object for the declaring class

public void foo()
{
  synchronized ( getClass() )
  {
    // ...
  }
}
```

If the synchronized block occurs inside a static method, there is no *this* on which the *getClass* method can be invoked. Instead, we have to obtain a reference to the *Class* object via the class literal. In general, this is worse than *getClass* because it involves a hard-coded reference to a class name that may change in the future:

```
// no 'this' receiver on which getClass() can be invoked, must use literal

public static void staticFoo()
{
  synchronized ( Foo.class )
  {
    // ...
  }
}
```

7.10 MUTEX OBJECT

It is usually preferable to invoke a *synchronized* method rather than execute a block *synchronized* on *this* because the code is a little cleaner. Sometimes however, a block synchronized on an object other than the receiver makes sense. A common Java idiom is to create a mutex object (for *mut*ual *ex*clusion). The mutex is typically the simplest object possible: a new instance of class *Object*. For example:

```
private Object mutex = new Object();

  // ...

public void foo()
{
  synchronized ( mutex )
  {
    // ...
  }
}
```

This completely internalizes the synchronization mechanism. If an external object synchronizes on the receiver, it will not interfere with the internal mutex synchronization as it would if the receiver synchronized on itself. Furthermore, this internal mutex gives fine-grained control over synchronization. A class may have more than one mutex to control different facets of its behavior. This approach can greatly increase the concurrency of an object. Instead of just having the one lock associated with itself, the object has multiple locks it can use to partition concurrent access.

In a variation of this idiom, the mutex is one of the *existing* fields of the object. For instance:

```
private List services = Collections.synchronizedList( new ArrayList() );

public void addService( IService service )
{
   services.add( service );
}

public void shutdown()
{
   synchronized ( services ) // synchronize on the list object
   {
      for ( Iterator i = services.iterator(); i.hasNext(); )
      {
         ( ( Service) i.next() ).shutdown();
      }
   }
}
```

Note that the *addService* method is not synchronized, because the *services.add* method is synchronized (we have a synchronized view on the list). Likewise, the *shutdown* method need not be *synchronized* because it can synchronize on the list explicitly. In this way, the thread-safety of the receiver is ensured by leveraging the thread-safety of a field.

7.11 DOUBLE-CHECKED LOCKING

Invoking synchronized methods is marginally more expensive than invoking non-synchronized methods. More importantly, if a method is unnecessarily synchronized, true thread parallelism (as can occur on multi-processor machines) is reduced due to the synchronization bottleneck. One common idiom for avoiding this synchronization overhead is **double-checked locking**. This simple idiom avoids synchronization with a short-circuiting check: The synchronization is skipped unless it is needed. Double-checked locking is especially relevant when the reason for the synchronization is for a very rare case. For example, it is commonly found in initialization code, as in the case of a lazy-initialized singleton. Synchronization is only needed in this case for the first few accesses to guarantee the instance is not initialized more than once. The following *Singleton* class employs this easy trick:

```
public class Singleton
{
  private static Singleton instance;

  public static Singleton getInstance()
  {
❶   if ( instance == null )
      initializeInstance();

    return instance;
  }

  private static synchronized void initializeInstance()
  {
❷   if ( instance == null )
      instance = new Singleton();
  }
}
```

Note that the *getInstance* method is not synchronized. This would be a problem without the locking employed later in the *initializeInstance* method. Indeed, it could result in multiple instantiations of the singleton. The check in ❶ prevents the synchronization. The check in ❷ is the double-check that prevents the common check-and-act race-condition.

The synchronization overhead is thus eliminated for all invocations except the first one (or the first few if the system is heavily concurrent).

7.12 INVOKING A METHOD ON ANOTHER THREAD

There are several ways to invoke a method on a separate thread: implement *Runnable*, extend *Thread*, create a *Runnable* or *Thread* helper class, or create an anonymous *Runnable*. The anonymous *Runnable* mechanism is presented here as it has emerged as the dominant idiom [Lea 1997a]. (The first approach, implementing *Runnable*, is typically reserved for active objects, see the section on active objects.) The idiom follows the following template:

```
// invoke bar on another thread
public void foo( final Object fooArg )
{
  Runnable runnable = new Runnable()
  {
    public void run() { bar( fooArg ); }
  };

  new Thread( runnable ).start();
}

private void bar( Object barArg )
{
  // ...
}
```

Note that in this approach, the instance variables of the containing class are available to the inner class. Likewise, final parameters to the containing method are automatically accessible to the inner method (without setting field values, or exposing data).

7.13 ACTIVE OBJECTS

An **active object** is an object that automatically runs itself on a new thread upon instantiation. There are two ways to create active objects:

1. extend *Thread*

2. implement *Runnable*

In general, extend *Thread* only if the class you are creating represents a kind of thread. For example, a *ReusableThread* in a thread pool is a kind of thread so it should extend *Thread*. If your class needs to have methods like *setPriority, setName, setDaemon*, and so forth, chances are it should extend *Thread*. All other active objects should implement *Runnable*. This gives active objects maximum freedom in inheritance. An active object looks like this:

```
public class ActiveObject implements Runnable
{
    private Thread myThread;

    public ActiveObject( Object arg1, int arg2 )
    {
        // initialization ...

        Thread myThread = new Thread( this );
        myThread.start();
    }

    public void run()
```

```
{
  if ( Thread.currentThread() == myThread )
  {
    // do work...
  }
 }
}
```

Active objects should be used when the thread creation should be completely encapsulated. Otherwise, see the section on invoking a method on another thread for an external threading mechanism. An example of an active object might be a *Server* class that models the server side of a network application. When instantiated, a *Server* might create a *ServerSocket* and a thread to listen for connections from that socket.

In general, an active object should retain a reference to its thread. This allows for graceful shutdown (see the thread termination section), and allows the *run* method to be guarded against external threads via the thread identity check. This prevents malicious (or inadvertent) re-invocation of the run method.

7.14 THREAD TERMINATION

Terminating a running thread is tricky business. However, most applications need to support this behavior. *Cancel* buttons often require it, clean resource reclamation demands it, and graceful VM exit often involves it. There are many techniques available, but few guarantee consistent behavior. The technique presented here uses a combination of *Thread.interrupt* and resource revocation [Lea 1997b].

There are three important thread states in the context of thread termination:

1. thread is suspended via one of *wait, sleep, join*

2. thread is executing code

3. thread is performing blocking I/O (e.g., socket read).

Each case presents different challenges that must be dealt with for effective thread termination. The first two states are handled with *Thread.interrupt*. The last state is handled with resource revocation in the form of closing the associated stream.

Thread.interrupt does two things: If the thread is waiting or sleeping, it ends the wait/sleep by throwing an exception on the receiver thread; it sets a flag on the receiver to indicate it has been interrupted. The exception guarantees that state one is handled, the flag guarantees that state two is handled. Because *InterruptedException* is best used by an application to indicate a termination condition, it should begin the process of graceful shutdown:

```
try
{
  wait();
}
catch( InterruptedException ex )
{
  shutdown(); // execute clean up logic
  return;     // or some other form of halt (e.g., rethrow ex)
}
```

If the thread is busy executing code, it should periodically check to see if it has been interrupted. There are two ways to do this: the static method *Thread.interrupted*, and the instance method *Thread.isInterrupted*. Both return a *boolean* to indicate if the thread has been interrupted, but the static method clears the flag. This can be an awkward side-effect if other parts of the application expect an interrupted thread to have the flag set. In general, *Thread.isInterrupted* is preferred. It can be accessed in the following way:

```
if ( Thread.currentThread().isInterrupted() )
{
   shutdown();
   return; // or otherwise halt
}
else
{
   performLongCalculation();
}
```

The issue of when to check the interrupted status is purely application dependent. In general, it should be checked before performing a lengthy calculation (especially if synchronized), before a blocking I/O call, before performing an undoable action, and before invoking *wait*. Even during a lengthy operation, it should be periodically checked. The frequency should be chosen so as not to significantly impact performance, but still allow a timely termination.

The last state (in which a thread is in the process of a blocking I/O operation) is a little trickier. The original intent of *Thread.interrupt* was to cause an *InterruptedIOException* in this case. Unfortunately, this has been an extremely difficult behavior to implement on some platforms, so it has never been fully implemented. It is doubtful that it ever will be implemented so it should not be trusted. Instead, the application should close the appropriate stream to allow the thread to proceed. It should still invoke *Thread.interrupt* so that the waking thread realizes the *IOException* caused by the *close* invocation is in fact a request to terminate, as illustrated in Listing 7.2.

Listing 7.2 Thread interruption.

```
   // logic in terminator thread

listenerThread.interrupt();
in.close();


   // logic in terminated thread

try
{
```

```
  int value = in.read();
}
catch( IOException ex )
{
  if ( Thread.currentThread().isInterrupted() )
  {
    // handle termination request
  }
  else
  {
    // handle transient I/O failure, may handle same as above...
  }
}
```

8 LIBRARY IDIOMS— COLLECTIONS

In this chapter

- Guidelines for using the Java 2 Collections framework.

Collection objects provide a mechanism to model one-to-many relationships. The Java Collections framework provides implementations optimized to many different variants of the one-to-many relationship, interfaces under which these implementation details can be hidden, and algorithms to operate on these interfaces in generic yet powerful ways. This chapter covers important, but perhaps less obvious aspects of the Collections framework (as is the theme of the book). See the performance chapters for performance tips related to Java 2 collections.

8.1 THE API

The Java Collections API, like most other Java APIs, is built around a few core interfaces. As is the case with all interfaces, they are meant to provide developers with an abstraction layer that can be used to hide implementation details. The Collections API also includes multiple implementations of the core interfaces.

Figure 8.1 The Collections framework API.

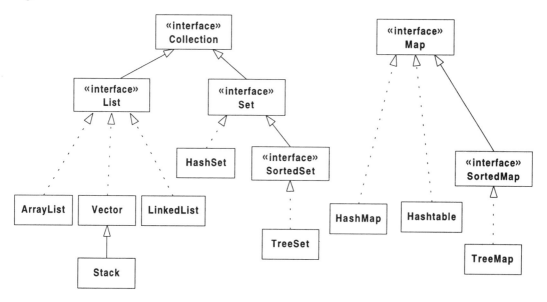

Notice that the *Map* hierarchy is completely independent of the *Collection* hierarchy. For this reason, the generic term **container** will be used here to refer to an object that may be a collection or a map.

The API is used most effectively when you program to interfaces, not implementations. This allows alternative implementations to be substituted without requiring modifications to the client code:

```
// BETTER, could substitute a LinkedList later...

List list = new ArrayList();

// WORSE

ArrayList list = new ArrayList();
```

8.2   STORING YOUR OWN OBJECTS IN CONTAINERS

Most container operations manipulate the contents of the container as instances of *java.lang.Object*. This means that the only methods available to the container for a given object are the methods in *Object*.

In particular, *Object.equals* is used as the basis of methods such as *List.contains*, *List.indexOf*, *Map.containsValue*, *Map.get*, *Map.put*, and so forth. These methods compare values within the container by invoking the *equals* method. Sometimes objects cannot get by with the default implementation of *equals* in *Object* (which is equivalent to ==). It is common to want to implement value-based equality. For example, two *Employee* objects don't have to be the same instance to be equal, rather they are equal if the IDs, names, or other attributes are equal. Overriding *equals* to return *true* when appropriate will ensure consistent and correct behavior for the container methods that depend on this functionality.

The fact that we override *Object.equals* puts yet another restriction on our class: We must override *Object.hashCode* as well. The reason is simple; the contract for all Java objects says that two objects that are equal must have the same hash code. Since we are overriding *equals* to return *true* when two distinct objects have the same value, we therefore need to override *hashCode* to return the same values for distinct objects that are equal.

Why does this contract exist? It exists to provide a mechanism for fast associative lookup. That is, it exists to support *HashMap* and other hashing containers. Instances of *HashMap* use *hashCode* methods as the first pass in determining the value to which a given key maps. Once the lookup has been narrowed down by this hashing process, the map then uses the *equals* method on the key to compare it to the keys it contains. This process forms the basis of the *HashMap.get*, *HashMap.put*, and *HashMap.remove* methods among others.

8.3 VIEWS AND VIEW IDIOMS

The Collections framework makes liberal use of the *Decorator* pattern [GHJV 1995]. Recall that decorators are objects that are used to transparently attach or modify behaviors of other objects. The decorators in the Collections framework are containers that wrap other containers to provide a modified **view** of the underlying container. In general, modifications to the underlying container are reflected in the view. If developers follow the *program to interface* idiom, the details of this view decorator object are hidden from the user.

COLLECTION-VIEWS FOR MAPS

Though *Map* does not extend *Collection*, it can be viewed as one. In fact, each of the three natural collection possibilities are available. A map can be viewed as a collection of keys, values, or key-value pairs.

The primary reason to view a map as a collection is to support iteration. Use the *Map.values* method to iterate over the collection-view of a map's values as in:

```
// Iterate over the value collection view of a map:

public void startupServices() throws StartupException
{
  for ( Iterator i = services.values().iterator(); i.hasNext(); )
  {
    ( (IService) i.next() ).startup();
  }
}
```

Likewise, the *Map.keySet* method can be used to iterate over the key collection-view of a map.

Iterating over the key-value collection-view is a slightly trickier (but thankfully, less frequently encountered) business. In this scenario, the *Map.entrySet* method is used to obtain a collection of *Map.Entry* objects (the peculiar name of which is due to the fact that the *Entry* interface is a public, named inner class of *Map*).

```
for ( Iterator i = employees.entrySet().iterator(); i.hasNext(); )
{
  Map.Entry e = (Map.Entry) i.next();
  System.out.println( e.getValue() + " has ID " + e.getKey() );
}
```

Note that it is often equivalent to iterate through the key set and use *Map.get* to access the value:

```
for ( Iterator i = employees.keySet().iterator(); i.hasNext(); )
{
   String id = (String) i.next();
   System.out.println( employees.get( id ) + " has ID " + id );
}
```

RANGE-VIEWS FOR LISTS

In Java 1, many methods that operated on *Vectors* also had to be written to operate on a particular range within the *Vector*.

```
// full-Vector version
public void putAllInCubicles( Vector employees )
{
   // ...
}

// and then there would be a range version
public void putAllInCubicles( Vector employees, int begin, int end )
{
   // ...
}


// typical invocations might be:
putAllInCubicles( employees );
putAllInCubicles( employees, Office.LEFT_WING, Office.RIGHT_WING - 1 );
```

With a range-view, there need be only a single version that accepts a list. A range-view of the list can be used to perform an operation on a range of the list. A range-view is a *List* object that is a sublist of the original list. Thus we have removed the need for special-case range operations; our methods simply operate on a list.

```
// implement a single version that accepts a List

public void putAllInCubicles( List employees )
{
  // ...
}
```

```
// use a range-view to operate on a portion of the list

putAllInCubicles( employees.subList( Office.LEFT_WING, Office.RIGHT_WING )
);
```

Range-views are used in this fashion to replace the *Vector.indexOf(Object, int)* method. The resulting code is slightly more involved:

```
// the Java 1 way

return vector.indexOf( employee, begin );

// the Java 2 way

int index = list.subList( begin, list.size() ).indexOf( employee );
return ( index < -1 ) ? -1 : index + begin;
```

Note that the value returned by *indexOf* on the sublist is the index of the object in the *sublist*.

SYNCHRONIZED-VIEWS

Most of the Java 2 collection implementations are not thread-safe. That is, they cannot be accessed safely from multiple threads. This is natural because thread synchronization overhead is often undesirable for situations where only one thread will be accessing the container at a given time. (In practice, this overhead is usually very small, especially with the HotSpot VM. However, it is also a general best practice to pay only for what you use.)

In those situations where you know you need thread safety, use one of the thread-safe views. These views are also called **synchronized-views** because most of the methods that operate on the container are *synchronized*. Synchronized-views of a container are easily retrieved from the *Collections* class through the *Collections.synchronized<type>* methods.

```
// synchronized-view of a list

private List list = Collections.synchronizedList( new ArrayList() );

  // synchronized-view of a map

private Map map = Collections.synchronizedMap( new HashMap() );

  // synchronized-view of a set

private Set set = Collections.synchronizedSet( new HashSet() );
```

(Note that the *Vector,* and *Hashtable* classes are also thread-safe versions of *List* and *Map* classes respectively. As such, they could be used as alternatives to the thread-safe views.)

Though the methods on synchronized container views are thread-safe, there is one important caveat: *Iteration* through a synchronized-view of a container is *not* thread-safe. Because of this, iteration through a container should be done in a synchronized block. For example, here is how to iterate through a list in a thread-safe way:

```
// assume services is a list of IService objects

synchronized ( services ) // synchronize on the list object
{
  for ( Iterator i = services.iterator(); i.hasNext(); )
  {
    ( ( Service) i.next() ).shutdown();
  }
}
```

Likewise, to perform a thread-safe iteration through one of the collection views of a map, wrap the iteration in a block that is synchronized on the *map* (as opposed to the collection-view of the map):

```
// assume services is a map of service IDs to IService objects

synchronized ( services ) // synchronize on the map
{
    for ( Iterator i = services.values().iterator(); i.hasNext(); )
    {
        ( (IService) i.next() ).shutdown();
    }
}
```

UNMODIFIABLE-VIEWS

The need often arises to have a collection that cannot be modified. The **unmodifiable-views** provide this capability. Unmodifiable-views wrap a collection and allow only the *read* methods (such as *size, get,* and so forth) to be invoked on the underlying collection. Write-methods (such as *put, remove,* and so forth) are implemented to throw *UnsupportedOperationException.* Like synchronized-views, unmodifiable-views are obtained from the Collections class through the appropriate *Collections.unmodifiable<type>* method.

There are two primary uses of unmodifiable-views. The first use is to provide read-only access to particular clients while retaining the ability to modify the container internally. An unmodifiable-view is used to wrap the underlying container. Clients get references to the unmodifiable-view while the internal reference is kept as an ordinary modifiable container.

```
/**
 * Our employees collection is an ordinary Set (probably a HashSet).
 * However clients of this method are not allowed to modify the
 * set itself so we give them an unmodifiable view.
 */
public Set getEmployees()
{
    return Collections.unmodifiableSet( employees );
}
```

The second use of unmodifiable-views is to support **immutable** containers. An immutable container is a container to which *all* references are through unmodifiable views. Typically, a standard modifiable container is created and populated. It is then wrapped in an unmodifiable-view. The unmodifiable-view is kept and the reference to the underlying container is discarded. Since no one will have a modifiable view to the container, the container will be immutable.

```
/**
 * When this method returns, the modifiable tempList view is lost
 * forever. Our only reference is to the unmodifiable-view called
 * statesInTheUnion. statesInTheUnion is therefore *immutable*.
 */
private void initializeStates()
{
  List tempList = new ArrayList();

  for ( int i = 0; i < NUM_STATES; i++ )
  {
    tempList.add( getState( i ) );
  }

  statesInTheUnion = Collections.unmodifiableList( tempList );
}
```

8.4 MANIPULATION IDIOMS

There are many uses of the Collections API that, while not immediately obvious, can simplify application code. Elegant solutions can be formed by skillful combinations of container operations. This section does not cover all of these techniques, but it does illustrate a thought process that you can use to discover container idioms of your own. Luckily, this technique has a single, simple principle: never code by hand what the collections framework has already coded for you

> Before coding a complex low-level routine, search the Collections framework for combinations of container operations that will simplify the code.

Consider the following example. There are two maps. We want to see if the second map is a submap of the first map. That is, we want to know if each key in the second map is found in the first map, and furthermore, whether the values to which the keys map are equal. The novice user of the Collections framework might set off to hand-code this logic and arrive at something similar to the following:

```
// WORSE

boolean isSubmap = true;

for ( Iterator i = second.keySet().iterator(); i.hasNext(); )
{
  Object key = i.next();
  Object valueInFirst = first.get( key );
  Object valueInSecond = second.get( key );

  if ( valueInSecond == null ) // watch out for NullPointerExceptions!
  {
    if ( valueInFirst != null )
    {
      isSubmap = false;
      break;
    }
  }
  else if ( !valueInSecond.equals( valueInFirst ) )
  {
    isSubmap = false;
    break;
  }
}
```

On the other hand, the more experienced user of the Collections framework would wonder if there is a simpler way. The thought process might go like this: "I want to know if the first map contains all of the entries in the second map. Hmmm, I wonder if there is a *contains* method on *Map*. Nope, only *containsKey* and *containsValue*, but I need to know if the key-value pairs from the second are contained in the first. Ahh! I can get the key-value pairs with the *entrySet* method. Wait! That's perfect because *entrySet* returns a *Set*, which is a *Collection*, and *Collection* has the *containsAll* method. I can see if the entry set of the first map contains all of the map entries of the second map."

The result of this thought process is that the abomination above is banished with the following *single line* of code:

```
// BETTER

boolean isSubmap = first.entrySet().containsAll( second.entrySet() );
```

Clearly, collection idioms can greatly improve our code. The following idioms, presented in the collections trail of *The Java Tutorial* [Bloch 1998], will get you started on your journey to master the collections framework.

Listing 8.1 Initialize a list to default values.

```
List list = new ArrayList( Collections.nCopies( 100, "Empty" ) );
```

Listing 8.2 Iterate backward through a list.

```
for ( ListIterator i = list.listIterator( list.size() ); i.hasPrevious(); )
{
  IService service = (IService) i.previous();
  // ...
}
```

Listing 8.3 Remove all occurrences of an element.

```
// Collection (removeAll takes a collection, so get singleton collection)

collection.removeAll( Collections.singleton( element ) );

// Map (remove all key-value pairs where value = element)

map.values().removeAll( Collections.singleton( element ) );
```

BINARY SEARCH THROUGH A SORTED LIST

If a list is sorted, a binary search will outperform an *indexOf* operation.

The index returned is awkward due to the fact that it serves as a double return value ("+" / "-" indicates found/not found, while the magnitude indicates position). Memorize this form:

```
// list must be sorted according to the natural ordering!

int index = Collections.binarySearch( list, object );

if ( index < 0 )
{
  list.add( -index - 1, object ); // add the object where it should be
}
```

9 LIBRARY IDIOMS— RESOURCES

In this chapter

- Idioms to use ResourceBundles to support internationalization and flexible configuration.

9.1 RESOURCEBUNDLE FOR LOCALIZATION

ResourceBundle is used as a mechanism of factoring locale specific code out of an application. This makes it easy to customize the application for other languages and cultures. Here are some examples:

■ Labels – GUI labels should be put into resource bundles so GUIs can be easily translated into other languages.

■ Icons – Icons should be placed in resource bundles so they may be substituted with icons that are more meaningful for other locales.

■ Exception Messages – Exception messages should be factored out so applications can be easily translated into other languages.

Resource bundles are easy to use, and necessary for internationalizing applications. In general, they are so easy to use that any significant application should use them for all localizable resources, even if an international audience is not expected. (Mainframe programmers didn't expect their code to be used 20 years later, and look where that practice got us.)

The most flexible resource bundle class in the JDK is the *ListResourceBundle*. Not only can list resource bundles contain any object, they can also be used in place of property resource bundles by factoring strings out into system properties.

One commonly encountered (and error-prone) misuse of resource bundles involves the use of duplicated string keys. For example:

```
// WORSE
import java.util.*;

public class AppResources extends ListResourceBundle
{
  private static Object[][] contents =
    {
      { "YES_LABEL", "Yes" },
      { "NO_LABEL", "No" },
    };

  public Object[][] getContents()
  {
    return contents;
  }
}
```

which is typically used as in:

```
❶ ResourceBundle res = ResourceBundle.getBundle( "AppResources" );
  JButton button = new JButton( res.getString( "YES_LABEL" ) );
```

What's wrong with this example? For one thing, the name of the resource bundle is typed in manually ❶. A class literal would guarantee compile-time verification of the resource bundle choice. Second, the *"YES_LABEL"* key is duplicated in the resource bundle class and the application itself. As new keys are introduced, and the namespace gets complicated, these key names may have to change. If the application is not changed to keep in perfect synchronization, a bug will have been introduced that can only be discovered at runtime. Luckily, both of these problems can be easily solved.

The following example demonstrates a well factored *ListResourceBundle*:

```
// BETTER

import java.util.*;

public class AppResources extends ListResourceBundle
{
  public static final String YES = "Yes";
  public static final String  NO = "No";

  private static Object[][] contents =
    {
      { YES, YES },
      { NO, NO },
    };

  public Object[][] getContents()
  {
    return contents;
  }
}
```

Application classes can access the resources defined in the resource bundle by the constants defined in the *AppResources* class:

```
// could optionally cache the resource bundle in a static field
// if used frequently

ResourceBundle res = ResourceBundle.getBundle(
    AppResources.class.getName() );

// typo-proof, and no string duplication

JButton button = new JButton( res.getString( AppResources.YES ) );
```

The first problem with our example is prevented by using a class literal to allow compile-time verification of our resource name. The second problem was fixed by defining constants in the *AppResources* class. By using constants, the application code does not need to know what the keys are, and use of *magic strings* is prevented. In fact, with this approach, the keys can be anything at all—it is the name of the key's field that conveys information to the developer. In this case it was convenient to define the keys to have the same value as the default resource values because those values were strings. If a resource value is not a string, the key can be defined as any *String* unique to the set of resource bundle keys.

```
public class AppResources_de extends AppResources
{

    private static Object[][] contents =
        {
            { YES, "Ja" },
            { NO, "Nein" },
        };

    // ...
```

> Define constants in the resource bundle for the resource keys and use these from the application.

Another common misuse of *ListResourceBundle* is to add locale independent information into the bundle. *ListResourceBundle* is a very flexible class. Though the keys must be of type *String*, the values can be any object. However, keep in mind that the purpose of a resource bundle is to factor out those elements of an application that are locale specific. Use this as the primary way to decide what to put in the resource bundle. Consider the following options for a list resource bundle's contents:

```
// BETTER (usually)

private static Object[][] contents =
   {
      { OK, OK },
      { CANCEL, CANCEL },
      { APPLY, APPLY }
   };

   // WORSE

private static Object[][] contents =
   {
      { OK, new JButton( OK ) },
      { CANCEL, new JButton( CANCEL ) },
      { APPLY, new JButton( APPLY ) }
   };
```

Both approaches are valid, but we claim the first is superior. The reason lies in the fact that for most applications, the GUI will use a button regardless of the locale. The second approach requires that subclasses create buttons just to override the button text. This complicates creation of the resource subclass, and does not foster reuse. Store complex objects in the resource only if it increases reuse, or simplifies code.

Maximize reuse when using resource bundles. In general, factor only locale-specific resources into resource bundles.

9.2 RESOURCEBUNDLE FOR SYSTEM PROPERTIES

Resource bundles can also be used to specify properties to an application. A Java VM can be initialized with a system property using the *–D* option as in:

```
java -Dcom.foo.factory=com.foo.security.SecureObjectFactory com.foo.Main
```

However, there is no convenient mechanism for specifying a file of multiple properties. Property resource bundles can be used to do this. A property file is created as usual. Consider the following:

```
# Simple property file named Foo.properties. Place this anywhere in
# the classpath (usually put in same Jar as the code)

material=Leather
color=Red
size=Large
```

This properties file is trivially accessed using the *ResourceBundle* class:

```
ResourceBundle props = ResourceBundle.getBundle( "Foo" );

for( Enumeration e = props.getKeys(); e.hasMoreElements(); )
{
    String key = (String) e.nextElement();
    System.setProperty( key, props.getString( key ) );
}
```

This example exports the properties to *System*. Some applications will not want to export the properties to *System*. They may prefer to use the properties directly, then discard them when done.

9.3 RESOURCE LOADING

Many applications have non-code resources, like sound and image files, that need to be loaded in a locale-dependent way. Java 2 provides the *Class.getResourceAs-Stream* method—among others—for loading these resources. When combined with resource bundles, developers have an easy way to localize applications for images, audio, and other complex resources.

```
// client lookup code

ResourceBundle b = ResourceBundle.getBundle( MyResource.class.getName() );
String audioFileName  = b.getString( MyResource.WARNING_AUDIO_FILE );
InputStream in = getClass().getResourceAsStream( audioFileName );

// verify 'in' is not null, then load the audio file...
```

Each localized version of the *MyResource* bundle is configured with a different file name for the warning audio file. For example:

```
public class MyResource
{
  public static final String WARNING_AUDIO_FILE = "/resources/warning.au";

  private static Object[][] contents =
    {
      { WARNING_AUDIO_FILE, WARNING_AUDIO_FILE }, // ...
    };

  // ...
```

```
public class MyResource_de extends MyResource
{
  private static Object[][] contents =
    {
      { WARNING_AUDIO_FILE, "/resources/achtung.au" }, // ...
    };

  // ...
```

In this scenario, the resources are looked up using absolute resource names. The Jar file containing the client class should contain a folder called *resources* in which the audio file resources are stored. The Java 2 class/resource loading mechanism will find the resource and return an input stream for it.

10 LIBRARY IDIOMS— EXCEPTIONS

In this chapter

- Common practices when implementing exception handling.

Exceptions are the linchpin of a robust Java application. When used effectively, they can greatly improve the stability (and often the understandability) of an application. And yet, there are a number of issues that must be dealt with in order to ensure they are being used correctly. For instance, the Java language gives us runtime exceptions and checked exceptions, but says little about when and how we should use one or the other. Likewise, there is nothing in the Java language to help us decide when to catch an exception and when to throw it. The following suggestions can answer these and other questions, and help you make the most of this powerful language feature.

10.1 CHECKED EXCEPTIONS VS. RUNTIME EXCEPTIONS

The difference between checked exceptions and runtime exceptions (exceptions that extend *RuntimeException*) is not that runtime exceptions occur at runtime. All exceptions occur at runtime. The difference is that the compiler verifies—that is, it *checks*— that checked exceptions are handled. It does not verify that runtime exceptions are handled. In the case of checked exceptions, the compiler ensures that the exceptions are either caught, or that the invoking method declares the exception in its *throws* clause.

At a design level, the difference between checked and runtime exceptions is that checked exceptions indicate *unpreventable* errors, and runtime exceptions indicate *preventable* errors. A runtime exception thus generally indicates a *programmer error*. Here are some examples:

Exception	Type	Justification
ArrayIndexOutOf-BoundsException	Runtime	Thrown when an attempt is made to access an array beyond its bounds. Programmer can prevent this by checking the array size.
ClassCastException	Runtime	Thrown when an illegal type cast is performed. Programmer can prevent this using *instanceof* operator.

Exception	Type	Justification
ClassNotFoundException	Checked	Thrown when *Class.forName* is used to load a class. Programmer cannot prevent the class from being removed from the system.
IllegalMonitorStateException	Runtime	Thrown when a *wait* or *notify* is invoked without first obtaining the monitor for an object. Programmer can prevent this by synchronizing on the object.
InterruptedException	Checked	Thrown when *Thread.interrupt* is invoked on a waiting, sleeping, or suspended thread. Programmer cannot prevent this method from being invoked.
IOException	Checked	Thrown when some I/O failure occurs. Programmer cannot, for instance, prevent network or disk failures.
NoSuchElementException	Runtime	Thrown when *Iterator.next* is invoked past the end of the iteration. Programmer can prevent by checking *Iterator.hasNext*.

Most user defined exceptions will fall into the category of unpreventable errors, and will therefore be defined as checked exceptions. The few cases that involve preventable errors often involve parameter validation, and are thus handled with *IllegalArgumentException*:

```
/**
 * Prevent NullPointerExceptions down the road...
 */
public void setName( String name )
{
  if ( name == null )
    throw new IllegalArgumentException( NULL_NAME_ERROR_MSG );

  this.name = name;
}
```

10.2 EMERGENCY ERROR HANDLER

Good applications are capable of handling expected errors gracefully, great applications are capable of handling unexpected errors gracefully. We like to build great applications—this means we must be prepared for all contingencies. We need an *emergency error handler*. Java gives us just such a mechanism in the *ThreadGroup.uncaughtException* method (see the Javadoc for this method). The *uncaughtException* method allows a *ThreadGroup* object to deal with all unhandled *Throwable* objects thrown on any of its threads. These *Throwable* objects are almost always instances of *Error* or *RuntimeException*.[1] The key to guaranteeing graceful handling

---

1. Java-language compliant compilers are supposed to guarantee that checked exceptions are ultimately dealt with. Oddly enough, this is a condition only in the Java language, and *not* in the Java VM. That is, the VM does not require checked exceptions to be caught or declared, so malicious or erroneous code generation can actually result in checked exceptions being thrown where a compiler would not allow it.

of unexpected errors is that all application threads must belong to a thread group customized to handle the error. This is not always possible, as in the case of applets where security restrictions may prevent the creation of new instances of *Thread-Group*.

The following *Main* class is written to extend *ThreadGroup* and handle all unexpected application exceptions. Note that all threads created from the application will belong to the custom threadgroup unless they are explicitly created in another threadgroup (as is the case for some system threads). Because of this, all unhandled exceptions occurring on application threads will wind up invoking the custom *uncaughtException* method.

```
public class Main extends ThreadGroup
{
  private Main()
  {
    super( "Application" );
  }

  public static void main( String[] args )
  {
    Runnable appStarter = new Runnable()
      {
        public void run()
        {
          // invoke method to start application...
        }
      };

    new Thread( new Main(), appStarter ).start();
  }

  public void uncaughtException( Thread t, Throwable ex )
  {
    // log error and display message or dialog
  }
}
```

The implementation of the *uncaughtException* method will differ for each application. Likewise the behavior will depend on the type and severity of the exception. An unrecoverable error might be cause for shutting down the application. A minor runtime exception might only be logged and ignored.

Because emergency error handling is such a valuable tool, we recommend this as the canonical form of a *Main* class.

10.3 TO CATCH OR TO THROW?

Each time we invoke a method that throws a checked exception we have to make the decision to catch the exception, or declare it in the throws clause of the invoking method. Here are the two options in action:

```
// catch exception

public void readName()
{
  try
  {
    name = in.readUTF();
  }
  catch( IOException ex )
  {
  // do something constructive
  }
}

// declare exception

public void readName() throws IOException
{
  name = in.readUTF();
}
```

It is not always easy to determine which option to take. Note that exception handling is like a method in that it is a form of responsibility. The *GRASP* responsibility assignment patterns help developers determine how to assign responsibilities such as exception handling [Larman 1997]. The general rule of thumb is to *catch the exception at the point closest to the occurrence of the exception that allows execution to proceed in a stable way.* In the example above, if the "do something constructive" code allows execution to proceed while retaining consistent objects (for example, if the *name* can be set to a default value) then catching close to the exception occurrence makes sense.

10.4 CONVERTING EXCEPTIONS

A common problem in object-oriented development is that of adapting one API to another. In a layered architecture, the exceptions of the lower layer will need to be caught and handled, or else they must be converted into exceptions applicable in the higher layer. This idiom is known as *Convert Exceptions* [ABW 1997].

For example, consider the case of cloning an object. There are many unpredictable exceptions that might occur during a clone. On the other hand *Object.clone* only throws one checked exception, *CloneNotSupportedException*. Therefore, if the *clone* operation fails due to a checked exception that is part of another API, this exception must be converted into a *CloneNotSupportedException*. Consider the following:

```
public Object clone() throws CloneNotSupportedException
{
  try
  {
    Foo other = (Foo) super.clone();
    other.setBar( bar.cloneReference() );
    return other;
  }
  catch( CloneNotSupportedException ex )
  {
    throw ex;
  }
  catch( RemoteException ex )
  {
    throw new CloneNotSupportedException( ex.getLocalizedMessage() );
  }
}
```

In this example, the *cloneReference* method is a remote invocation subject to the rules of RMI in that it must throw *RemoteException*. On the other hand, clone can only throw *CloneNotSupportedException*. The solution is to catch *RemoteException*, obtain a localized version of its message, and create a new *CloneNotSupportedException* with that message.

Note that some exceptions—particularly those thrown from within the JDK—may not be initialized with a message. In these cases, it may be better to use the *toString* form of the exception. Alternatively, the exceptions may be nested if the "outer" exception has a constructor that accepts an exception. In all cases, the goal is to provide as much relevant information possible for debugging purposes.

```
try
{
  server.login( username, password );
  // ...
}
catch( RemoteException ex )
{
  throw new ServerUnavailableException( ex );
}
```

11 LANGUAGE IDIOMS

In this chapter

■ Idioms related to Java language features, such as inner classes and static initializer blocks.

This chapter provides an introduction to some idioms and practices of experienced Java developers that emphasize *language* aspects of Java, as opposed to idioms related to the Java libraries. This includes practices related to constructs using keywords, syntax, and control structures.

For example, suppose you have been exposed to the inner class construct. Next, it is useful to know the idiomatic uses of inner classes in Java, such as to define *Iterator* and *Enumeration* implementation classes for the outer class, *Runnable* implementations, or as *Pluggable Behavior Object* parameters. This chapter explores these common idioms.

Similar to the library idiom chapters, the objective here is to share common practices regarding language features that are *not obvious* to someone relatively new to Java, in order to help you accelerate mastery of Java. It is *not* our objective to repeat an explanation of language and library features that are straightforward from their introduction.

Our decision about what is "not obvious" is based on our experience as Java teachers working with many hundreds of software developers, and also as users ourselves of Java and Java literature. Here are some contrasting examples of what is and is not in the chapter:

Usage relatively obvious from definition or introductory example:

- The use of *interfaces* to define a set of operations that classes should implement is straightforward; thus, this is not discussed.

- The definition of *static initializer blocks* to initialize static variables is evident; thus, this is not stressed.

Idiomatic usage not self-evident from definition or introductory example:

- The definition of *interfaces* does not self-evidently reveal that they are idiomatically used to group together constants shared by a subsystem (or package) into one interface with only variables, but with no operations; thus, this is discussed.

- The definition of *static initializer blocks* does not self-evidently reveal that they are idiomatically used to load native libraries when there are native methods, or to register with another object when the class is loaded; thus, this is discussed.

11.1 INTERFACES

DECLARE SHARED CONSTANTS IN INTERFACES

When a variable is defined in an interface, then all implementing classes inherit it as a constant field. Therefore, it is considered good practice to organize shared constant definitions in interfaces. For example, the *java.beans.BeanInfo* interface specifies the constants used for indicating the appropriate graphical display characteristics.

```java
package java.beans;

interface BeanInfo        // our simplified version
{
   int ICON_COLOR_16x16 = 1;
   int ICON_COLOR_32x32 = 2;
   int ICON_MONO_16x16  = 3;
   int ICON_MONO_32x32  = 4;

   BeanDescriptor getBeanDescriptor();

   // ...
}
```

A method in an implementing class can refer to these constants directly (and any class can refer to the constants by qualifying them with the interface name).

```java
import java.beans.*;
import java.awt.*;

public class MyBeanInfo implements BeanInfo
{

   public Image getIcon( int iconKind )
   {
      Image img = null;

      switch( iconKind )
      {
         case ICON_COLOR_16x16:
            img = loadImage( "myicon_c16_16.gif" );
            break;

         // ...
```

A variation on this is a constants-only interface. It is customary to group function-ally related constants needed by a package or subsystem into an operation-less interface. Classes implement the interface in order to inherit the constants.

```
interface IColorCodes
{
   int RED   = 1;
   int GREEN = 2;
   int BLUE  = 3;
}
```

MARKER INTERFACES

An interface may have no operations—*java.io.Serializable* is an example. This is known as a **marker interface** or **tagging interface**.

```
interface Serializable {}
```

This idiom can be used when a design—usually a subsystem or framework—needs to simply test for set membership. This is usually done with an *instanceof* test. The serialization support provided by *java.io.ObjectOutputStream* is an example:

```
   // in class ObjectOutputStream (our simplified version)
public void writeObject( Object object )
{
   // ...
☞ if ( object instanceof Serializable )
   // ...
}
```

Another example is *java.rmi.Remote*.

```
interface Remote {}
```

All remote interfaces must extend this marker interface. (Note that polymorphism is usually referred to type-checking, but is not applicable here as the behavior is being externalized from the object.)

ENUMERATED TYPE OBJECTS VERSUS INTERFACE CONSTANTS

Enumerated type objects (or simply **enumerated types**) are used to declare a fixed range of values represented as constant objects, and as such can be used as an alternative to interface constants. The implementation has the following features:

- The class has no methods; it exists simply to represent a distinguished set of instances.

- The constructor is made *private*, so there is no chance of creating more instances.

- The class has a set of *public static final* fields that reference instances of the class.

For example:

```
// enumerated types
public final class ColorCode
{
    public static final ColorCode RED   = new ColorCode();
    public static final ColorCode GREEN = new ColorCode();
    public static final ColorCode BLUE  = new ColorCode();

    private ColorCode() {}
}
```

Contrast this with a typical interface-constants approach using *int* values:

```
// interface constants
```

```
interface IColorCodes
{
  int RED    = 1;
  int GREEN  = 2;
  int BLUE   = 3;
}
```

Disadvantages

One disadvantage of the enumerated type is its implementation. It is slightly, though not objectionably, cumbersome.

Another minor disadvantage is that enumerated types are slightly more awkward to use than interface constants. The latter are more easily accessible within a class by simply implementing the interface. That is, by implementing the interface a class has direct access to the constants. (We will see a solution to this problem in the following *Variations* sections). To contrast:

```
// if class Pencil implements the IColorCodes interface,
// access is direct

pencil.setColor( RED );

// not so with the enumerated type

pencil.setColor( ColorCode.RED );
```

Another very minor disadvantage lies in the memory overhead associated with objects versus primitives. The overhead of a few simple objects is not meaningful, but if the objects are regularly being converted to primitive values—as might happen in a wire protocol—then the marshalling overhead might be significant.

Advantages

The advantages associated with enumerated type objects probably outweigh the advantages of interface *int* constants. First, the enumerated type is type-safe. The only possible enumerated type values are those declared in the body of the enumerated type. Not so with interface constants. In our example, the compiler ensures that the only possible parameters to the *Pencil.setColor(ColorCode)* method are: *ColorCode.RED*, *ColorCode.GREEN*, and *ColorCode.BLUE*. There are no other possible *ColorCode* objects in existence because only the *ColorCode* class can instantiate new instances. The class is final, the constructor is private, and only RED, GREEN, and BLUE objects have been created. On the other hand, the compiler cannot catch the following erroneous usage of the *int* version *Pencil.setColor(int)*:

```
// 4 is a valid int, but not a valid color

pencil.setColor( 4 );
```

Another advantage is traceability. When planning to use *Pencil.setColor(ColorCode)*, a developer can note this from the parameter type and look up the *ColorCode* class to determine the permissible values. If *Pencil.setColor* accepts an *int*, then we have to rely on documentation to describe the permissible values, or be directed to read the *ColorCode* interface.

Lastly, note that comparison of the enumerated type constants can be efficiently performed with == because each *ColorCode* instance is at a different location.

```
if ( color == ColorCode.RED )
   System.out.println( "The color is red." );
```

Variations

Why not define the enumerates type objects in an interface, such as the following?

```
// enumerated types

interface IColorCodes
{
   ColorCode RED    = new ColorCode();
   ColorCode GREEN  = new ColorCode();
   ColorCode BLUE   = new ColorCode();
}
```

This is technically possible, but it suffers from the disadvantage of a loss of type safety. One may still create (elsewhere) other instances of the *ColorCode* (because this approach requires the *ColorCode* constructor to be public), which the original design avoids by making the constructor private.

A solution that combines the advantage of interface inheritance of the codes, with the advantage of type safety, is to place the interface and code class in a small package together, and make the constructor of the code class have package level visibility, so that only the interface can create instances. This is illustrated in the following listing.

```
package colorCodes;

interface IColorCodes
{
   ColorCode RED   = new ColorCode();
   ColorCode GREEN = new ColorCode();
   ColorCode BLUE  = new ColorCode();
}
```

```
package colorCodes;

public final class ColorCode
{
     // package-visible constructor

   ColorCode() {}
}
```

11.2 Inner Classes

Anonymous Inner Classes for *Runnable* Objects

Suppose that we wish to invoke the *runForever* method of the *Clock* class starting on a new thread, but the *Clock* class does not implement the *Runnable* interface, and we either can not or do not wish to make it implement this interface (for example, we may not have the source code).

```
public class Clock
{
  public void runForever()
  // ...
}
```

In this situation, it is common to define an anonymous inner class instance (as the parameter to the *Thread* constructor) that does implement *Runnable*, and which invokes the method on a new thread.

```
public class Configurator
{
  public void startClock()
  {
    Thread t = new Thread( new Runnable()
      {
        public void run()
        {
          new Clock().runForever();
        }
      } );

    t.start();
  }

  // ...
}
```

PRIVATE INNER CLASSES FOR ITERATOR IMPLEMENTATIONS

When an outer class contains a collection of objects that should be available for iteration, a private inner class is usually used to define the *java.util.Iterator* (or *Enumeration*) object. This is the style used in the JDK Collections Framework. In addition, we can apply this approach when defining new types that implement the Collections interfaces (such as *List*), or when defining any class for which we wish to provide an iterator, such as for the *AbstractSyntaxTree* illustrated in Listing 11.1.

Listing 11.1 Private inner class for Iterator implementation.

```
public final class AbstractSyntaxTree
{
  // ...

  public Iterator iterator()
  {
    return new ASTIterator();
  }

  private class ASTIterator implements Iterator
  {
    // ...

    public boolean hasNext() { /* */ }
    public Object next() { /* */ }
    public void remove() { /* */ }
  }
}
```

ANONYMOUS INNER CLASSES FOR PLUGGABLE BEHAVIOR OBJECTS

Pluggable Behavior [Beck 1997] is a popular pattern to parameterize the behavior of an object. It has many variations and is often seen in use to handle events in the delegation event model, and to parameterize operations in the ObjectSpace Java Generic Library (JGL), a popular (free) container library for Java included with most Java IDEs. A key idea of *Pluggable Behavior* is to plug in something that represents one behavior or one method into an object whose behavior can be parameterized. It is a central technique to implement *instance-specific* varying behavior, in addition to the *State* and *Strategy* patterns [GHJV 1995].

The implementation of *Pluggable Behavior* is idiosyncratic to each object-oriented programming language. For example, it is realized in Smalltalk using *blocks* or the standard library *perform* method, and in C++ using *templates, function pointers* or instances of the standard library *mem_fun1_t* class.

There are two common variations of its implementation in Java.

- It can be achieved with interfaces and anonymous inner classes to define and plug in the behavior. This is similar to Beck's *Pluggable Block* pattern for Smalltalk [Beck 1997]. Also known as *Pluggable Behavior Object*.

- *Pluggable Behavior* can be implemented with the Java Reflection API using *Method* objects and the *Method.invoke* operation. This is Beck's *Pluggable Selector* pattern [Beck 1997]. Also known as *Pluggable Method*, it is explored in the library idioms chapter covering uses of the Reflection API.

Pluggable Behavior Objects

In the *Pluggable Behavior Object* variation of pluggable behavior, anonymous inner classes are typically used to define objects with one behavior.

To start, here is a classic Java example of pluggable behavior object using anonymous inner classes for event handling. We can "plug in" the event handling behavior on the *JButton*.

The parameter to the *addActionListener* method is any object that implements the *ActionListener* interface and thus its one public method—*actionPerformed*. In this example, we define a lightweight pluggable behavior object that fulfills this contract, and pass it in as a parameter. Observe the signature quality of a behavior object: It is a simple object that represents one method.

Listing 11.2 A pluggable behavior object.

```
private void initialize()
{
  JButton button1 = new JButton( "Update" );
  button1.addActionListener( new ActionListener()
    {
      public void actionPerformed( ActionEvent evt )
      {
        // handle the ActionEvent
      }
    } );

  // ...
}
```

As an aside, in the case of event handlers and JavaBeans, the major Java IDEs contain Bean visual programming tools that will automatically generate these anonymous inner class event handlers based on "programming by wiring" and visual manipulation of iconic representations of Beans.

The JGL uses pluggable behavior objects to specify what action to perform on each element in a collection, during iteration operations. For example, the parameter to the *Filtering.reject* method is any object that implements the *UnaryPredicate* interface and thus its one public method—*execute*. Once again, we use an anonymous inner class to define a lightweight pluggable behavior object that fulfills this contract, and pass it in as a parameter.

Again, note the signature quality of a behavior object: It is a very simple object that represents one method.

Listing 11.3 A pluggable behavior object.

```
private Container getAllNonSystemClassesFor( Container classes )
{
    // JGL Filtering.reject returns a new Container that contains
    // all the elements of "classes" except those that cause
    // UnaryPredicate.execute to return true.

  return Filtering.reject( classes, new UnaryPredicate()
    {
      public boolean execute( Object element )
      {
        String className = (String) element;
        return
          className.startsWith( "java" ) ||
```

```
            className.startsWith( "javax" ) ||
            className.startsWith( "Ljava" );
        }
    },
    );
}
```

From these examples we see that a common pattern in Java when implementing *Pluggable Behavior Object* is to define an interface with a single operation, and to pass anonymous inner class instances as parameters. A following partial implementation of the *Filtering.reject* method illustrates this. Notice the use of the pluggable behavior object at ❶ in Listing 11.4.

```
interface UnaryPredicate
{
   boolean execute( Object element );
}
```

Listing 11.4 Using a pluggable behavior object.

```
public final class Filtering
{
   public Container reject( Container cont, UnaryPredicate predicate )
   {
      // ...

      for ( Iterator i = cont.iterator(); i.hasNext(); )
      {
❶        if ( !predicate.execute( i.next() ) )
         {
            // ...
         }
      }
   }

   // ...
}
```

A word of caution with respect this pattern: If many pluggable behavior objects are being rapidly created and destroyed, performance will be affected, since object creation and reclamation are not cheap. Also, if many different inner classes are written, there may be an opportunity to share code between them. To do this, put the shared code in method(s) in the containing class, and have the inner class objects invoke these methods.

11.3 STATIC INITIALIZERS

Static initializer blocks execute when a class is first loaded, in contrast to instance initializer blocks and constructors, which execute when an instance is created.[1]

STATIC INITIALIZER LOADS NATIVE LIBRARY

When a class contains native methods, static initializers are typically used to load the dynamic libraries that implement the methods.

```
public class StaticInitializers
{
  static
  {
    System.loadLibrary( "Library1" );

    // ...
  }


  public native void foo();

  // ...
}
```

---

1. As a point of Java trivia, instance initializer blocks are copied into the beginning section of each constructor when the class is compiled.

STATIC INITIALIZER PERFORMS REGISTRATION

When registration with another component needs to occur after class loading, a static initializer is commonly used. For example, JDBC drivers register with the *DriverManager* in this manner.

```java
import java.sql.*;

public class MyJDBCDriver implements Driver
{
  static
  {
    DriverManager.registerDriver( new MyJDBCDriver() );

    // ...
  }

  // ...
}
```

STATIC INITIALIZER WHEN STATIC FIELD EXCEPTION HANDLING

When a static field needs to be initialized to an object whose constructor throws a checked exception, a static initializer is usually used.

```java
import java.io.*;

public class StaticInitializers
{
  private static ObjectOutput out;
  private static String OUT_FN = "out.ser";

  static
  {
    try
    {
      out = new ObjectOutputStream( new FileOutputStream( OUT_FN ) );
    }
    catch( Exception ex )
    {
```

```
    , // ...
    }
  }
  // ...
}
```

STATIC INITIALIZERS FOR STATIC FIELD COMPLEX INITIALIZATION

In addition to the above examples, sometimes a static variable requires complex initialization, such as a collection that must be initialized with values from an external source. Static initializers can provide this service.

11.4 CONSTRUCTORS

DO CONSTRUCTOR CHAINING FROM LEAST TO MOST COMPLEX SIGNATURE

If a class has set of constructors, ranging from a default constructor to one with many parameters, the simpler constructors should, if possible, invoke their next most complex constructor, passing in appropriate default values. This minimizes duplication of initialization code. It is also considered good style to provide a range of constructors so that the user has choices in the degree of custom initialization.

```java
import java.math.*;

public class Money
{
   private Currency    currency;
   private BigDecimal amount;


   public Money()
   {
     this( new BigDecimal( 0 ) );
   }


   public Money( BigDecimal amount )
   {
     this( new Currency( "USA" ), amount );
   }


   public Money( Currency currency, BigDecimal amount )
   {
     this.currency = currency;
     this.amount = amount;
   }

   // ...
}
```

11.5 THE INSTANCEOF OPERATOR

IF POSSIBLE, TEST TO AN INTERFACE

Interface-based design is in general a Good Thing, because it allows for the flexible inclusion of different implementations. One way to support this paradigm is to, whenever possible, perform *instanceof* tests to an interface rather than a class. Of course, type tests in general are often a symptom of an undesirable design; look to replace type tests with solutions based on polymorphism, if possible.

```
// BETTER, assuming IAddress is an interface
if ( x instanceof IAddress ) ...
```

```
// WORSE, assuming Address is a class
if ( x instanceof Address ) ...
```

11.6 ACCESS MODIFIERS

HOW TO USE THE MODIFIERS

Private—This should be the default visibility of fields, with the exception of constants, in order to promote encapsulation. Also used for the visibility of helper methods not publicly invoked. As covered in the performance chapter, private methods increase the opportunity for compiler optimization by inlining.

Default (Package)—Most Java developers consider it good practice to avoid using default visibility for fields because it can lead to violation of encapsulation. Some developers (notably Sun) do typically use it for instance fields, but still treat them as *private* in practice; thus *private* could in essence have been used.

Protected—Do not use *protected* visibility for fields, because it breaks encapsulation in relation to subclasses. However, it is useful for methods in a class hierarchy that only subclasses should have access to. In the context of the *Template Method* design pattern, the *hook methods* are often protected [GHJV 1995].

Public—In addition to public operations, constants may be public.

11.7 CASTING

USUALLY INCLUDE TESTS WHEN CASTING

A recommended practice is to include a test or exception handling when casting a parameter or return value. For example:

- An *instanceof* test before attempting to cast.

- Catching a *ClassCastException*.

A common exception to this is casting the return values from collections—most developers do not consider it worthwhile to include tests or error handling because an error is so rare, and this very common construct would become fussy to write. Of course, safety-critical software is an exception.

If the likelihood of an incorrect cast or a null value is low, then as discussed in the performance chapter, performance is *marginally* improved by catching the error with exception handling rather than with explicit *instanceof* tests.

11.8 THE FINAL KEYWORD

FINAL TO PROMOTE INLINED METHODS

As discussed in the performance chapter, a compiler can in some circumstances inline methods, and thereby improve performance. If a method is declared *final*, this is a hint that the compiler (or a JVM) may use to consider inlining it. Similarly, if a class is declared *final*, many of its methods may be candidates for inlining.

12 PACKAGING IDIOMS

In this chapter

- Guidelines for physical organization of types in Java packages.

- Common case practices.

- Guidelines when there are many developers sharing a common large code base.

This chapter starts with fairly common practices that Java developers use to define packages.

It concludes with some less-known, but still useful, packaging tips. The goal is to create a robust physical design for a Java application or framework in terms of package definitions and the organization of types within packages.

There are two cases to consider:

1. (common case) Package organization when there is minimal impact of the organization on team development.

2. (less common case) Package organization when there are many developers sharing a common massive code base.

12.1 THE COMMON CASE

These guidelines are satisfactory for most development cases. They are easier to apply, but may produce a non-optimal design if there is a *very* large code base shared by *many* developers.

ORGANIZE TO REFLECT FUNCTIONALLY COHESIVE VERTICAL AND HORIZONTAL SLICES

Most relatively complex systems are designed in terms of layers which emphasize a *functional* separation of concerns, such as user interface, "domain" application logic, general services, and technical infrastructure; this is the *Layers* architecture pattern [BMRSS 1996]. For example, a system may be designed in vertical layers as illustrated in Figure 12.1. In addition, one layer is often divided into horizontal slices that group elements into finer sets, such as "domain—types related to insurance policies" and "domain—types related to customers."

This organization is a factoring based on **functional cohesion**—types are grouped together that are strongly related in terms of their participation in a common purpose, collaborations, policy, and function. For example, all the types in the JDBC *java.sql* package are related to the purpose of reading and writing a data source that understands SQL.

Finally, another commonly recommended packaging strategy is to place a family of related interfaces in a separate package by themselves. The EJB package *javax.ejb* is an example.

These packages are usually the basic unit of development work and of release. That is, the smallest unit of work assigned to one developer is often a package. In addition, in the context of team development, version control and configuration management, the package is the normal unit of release for shared use, rather than an individual class.

Listing 12.1 Sample layered design—packages and subpackages only, not types in packages.[1]

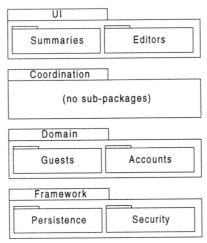

Java packages are often defined to reflect this logical structure; in the following examples, note the hierarchical naming pattern that reflects the logical categories.

Package names normally start according to the Sun recommended conventions of <domain>.<organization>, such as:

```
package com.icbm.<the rest>;
```

If the code is related to a particular project, the project name usually follows:

```
package com.icbm.reservations.<the rest>;
```

---

1. Note that in the UML packages are visualized as tabbed folders.

Common Package Name Categories

Common naming idioms for business information systems follow something like the conventions shown in Listing 12.2.

Listing 12.2 Common package categories.

Package Category	Description
coordination	Types that coordinate interaction between the UI and other layers. Types in this layer typically represent "controllers" or use case instances.
domain	Types whose names reflect domain concepts, and that are responsible for application logic related to these concepts.
framework	Types in a framework that collaborate to provide a service, and that may be extended by other application programmers, such as by subclassing and overriding methods.
service	Types in a "subsystem" that collaborate to provide a service, but which is not extendible like a framework.
ui	Types in the user interface, such as subclasses of Swing components (*JFrame*, *JPanel*, and so on).
util	Utility types that have no relationship, or only a very loose relationship between each other.

For example:

```
package com.icbm.reservations.ui;

package com.icbm.reservations.domain;
```

If the major package category contains many types, with smaller cohesive families, a further subdivision into minor categories is common, such as:

```
package com.icbm.resevations.ui.summaries;

package com.icbm.reservations.domain.guests;
```

One force against a too-fine grained decomposition of packages is if they are being used by other developers. For ease of recall and use, developers tend to prefer larger, fewer packages. However, as discussed in the next section, large packages can lead to problems on massive projects with many developers.

Utilities and frameworks are often usable across an organization, and thus it is common to not relate them to a particular project, but rather to name them to reflect their broader applicability:

```
package com.icbm.util.jdbc;

package com.icbm.framework.security;
```

Another basic heuristic in Java packaging is that if a functionally cohesive group of types is subservient to, and very dependent on another package, then name it as a "sub-package" of the "super-package." For example, *java.awt.event* contains all the delegation event model events that are used in *java.awt*. Similarly, *java.awt.image* contains the types for creating and modifying images within the AWT. Further, *java.awt.image.renderable* contains the types for rendering images.

The above guidelines are sufficient for most packaging design. However, in some rare cases, when there are dozens of developers simultaneously working on a massive *shared* code based (say, thousands of types), then the above design can be the cause of problems discussed in the following section.

12.2 THE LESS COMMON CASE—VERY LARGE TEAM DEVELOPMENT

The following issues and guidelines only need to be seriously considered during the development of very large Java systems with many developers. Otherwise, the potential problems raised in this section are not likely to materialize; and thus applying these more complex, fussy guidelines would not be worth the effort, and would result in an *over-engineered* design. In short, don't bother with this section unless you have to...

Consider this scenario: A Java development team of fifty developers is using a version control tool and shared code repository. Jill is responsible for package X, which is one of the most depended-on packages in the system. Every time Jill re-releases another version of package X, the other developers need to synchronize their version of package X to ensure they pick up her changes. In addition, the changes in package X may break code in other packages, initiating a transitive dependency impact—changes ripple across the package structure.

If many of the fifty developers are iteratively refining and releasing widely shared packages, the overall effect is something close to **version control thrashing**—an inordinate amount of time is spent by the team just synchronizing with each other's changes.

Consequently, if package X is widely depended upon, it is undesirable for it to be unstable and going through many new versions, since it increases the impact on the other developers in terms of version synchronization.

The excellent work of Robert Martin, who has done extensive investigation into physical design and packaging of C++ applications (some of which is applicable to Java), influenced several of the following guidelines that have emerged for Java. Please see [Martin 1995] for a C++ treatment of the subject; although be aware that some of the issues and the painstaking factoring required in C++ are unnecessary in Java, because C++ has delicate compile and link time dependencies that Java thankfully avoids.

Package as Unit of Release

An important assumption that underlies this discussion is this: For software developers working together on a project, the fundamental unit of release (to the developers) of a stable software entity is a *package*, not a type.

This is because types in a package tend to be used together, and often have dependencies on each other that require one to release them as a group. Additionally, re-releasing a single type (class or interface) is so fine-grained that it will cause an excessive rate of impact and *vexatious version synchronization* for other developers—and no one wants a vexed software engineer.

PHYSICAL DESIGN

What we are talking about is an aspect of **physical design**. While simply diagramming a design on a whiteboard or CASE tool, we can arbitrarily place types in any logically cohesive package without significant impact. But during *physical* design—the organization of types into physical units of release as Java packages—our choices will have significant influence on the degree of developer impact when changes in those packages occur, if there are many developers sharing a common code base.

OUR GOAL: REDUCING CHANGE DEPENDENCY

As the introductory scenario with Jill Programmer suggested, very large team development can lead to a state of version control thrashing, which is caused by high dependency on many unstable packages.

Thus, the solution is to design to *reduce* change dependency impact during development—reducing the impact when team members continually re-release new versions of packages during development of a system.

One of the mechanisms to meet this goal is to organize types in packages so that the majority of **expected** changes do not propagate widely when a package is re-released. The following guidelines provide ways to achieve this.

NOTATION—UML PACKAGE DIAGRAM

In order to analyze suitable package organization, dependencies between packages are shown with a dashed arrow line from the dependent to the depended-on package. In the following package diagrams, packages with the least dependency (on other packages) are shown at the top of the diagram, as illustrated in Figure 12.1.

The motivation for this organization is that we will strive to define the least-dependent packages as containing mostly *abstract* types (interfaces and abstract classes). Thus, the familiar type hierarchy structure of abstract types at the top of a diagram is mirrored in the package diagrams with abstract packages at the top. Conversely, some designers prefer to reverse the order, which is also acceptable.

Figure 12.1 Example of dependencies between packages.

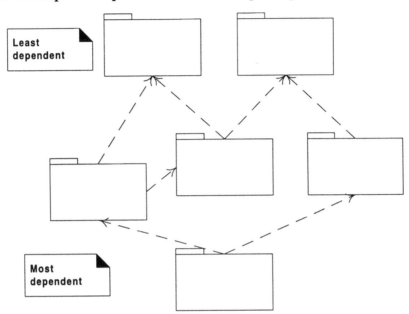

INTRODUCTION TO THE GUIDELINES

Here is the key problem, summarized: If the most depended-on packages are re-released frequently, then the most *dependent* packages in the dependency hierarchy will probably also require frequent re-release, because of propagating impact from the packages they depend on.

Since constant instability throughout the package structure is undesirable, several of these guidelines examine how to organize types in packages to avoid this.

In preparation, these definitions are used in later discussion:

- **Free**—a package with no dependents. It is free to change without affecting others. Its opposite is:

- **Responsible**—a package with many dependents.

- **Independent**—a package with no dependencies. Its opposite is:

- **Dependent**—a package with many dependencies (perhaps transitively).

Figure 12.2 Ideal package organization.

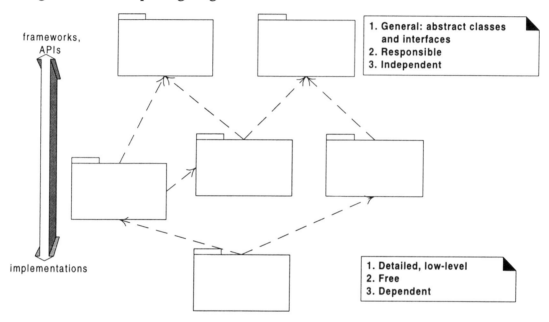

GUIDELINE: GRIN AT THE TOP

A fundamental principle of package organization is to make the most responsible (depended-on) types be general (abstract) and independent.

As a mnemonic aid: *GRIN at the top* (General, Responsible, and INdependent).

Figure 12.2 illustrates this ideal.

The motivation for this advice is that general and independent packages are more stable, and it is desirable for the most responsible packages to be stable.

The packages near the top of the diagram (general, responsible, independent) are most likely to represent frameworks and general utilities; the packages near the bottom represent implementations and clients of frameworks and utilities.

General, abstract types, such as abstract classes and interfaces are inherently less likely to change, since they do not contain much code, and they are very generalized.

Independent types have no external dependencies, and thus are *not* forced to change because of code instability elsewhere.

If the most responsible packages are quite stable, then these influential packages will seldom cause propagating change impact across other packages; this is good. Therefore, organize packages so that the most depended upon packages are stable; they will be more stable if they contain abstract types and very general components.

There are valid exceptions to this guideline. Sometimes very responsible packages are not abstract, as is discussed in the next section.

GUIDELINE: DON'T DEPEND ON MORE CONCRETE PACKAGES

This guideline could be viewed as a corollary of *GRIN at the top*, but it is worth being mindful of it as a distinct goal:

> Details should depend on abstractions, but abstractions should not depend on details.
>
> That is, a package of more abstract types should not have dependencies on a package of more concrete types.
>
> If a package of abstractions does depend on a package of more concrete types, redesign them both so that they both depend on a new common set of abstractions.

Figure 12.3 illustrates applying this principle to redesign a package structure. The result in this example is the JDBC architecture; the figure shows a before-and-after view. Admittedly, the flaw in the original design of this example is obvious to an experienced designer, but the point is to use a simple example, and remember to apply it to more subtle cases.

Suppose we had a Persistent Storage Services (PSS) package that was directly coupled to classes in a package to access "DB-Foo" brand relational databases (from "ICBM" Corp.). Assume the PSS was designed to be relatively general, and that one could plug in different relational databases, not just a DB-Foo database. Then it is undesirable to couple the PSS directly to the DB-Foo package—a more abstract package is dependent on a more concrete one.

A prime reason this is undesirable is that concrete packages tend to be less stable than more abstract packages; this increases the fragility of the design.

The solution is to create a new set of abstractions, such as the *java.sql* package of concepts including *Connection* and *Statement*, which both original packages depend on. The DB-Foo classes will implement the interfaces in *java.sql*, and the PSS will only know about the abstractions in *java.sql*. Of course, the JDK already provides the JDBC package for this specific example, but the general pattern applies when refactoring families of packages.

Figure 12.3 Redesign to avoid depending on more concrete types.

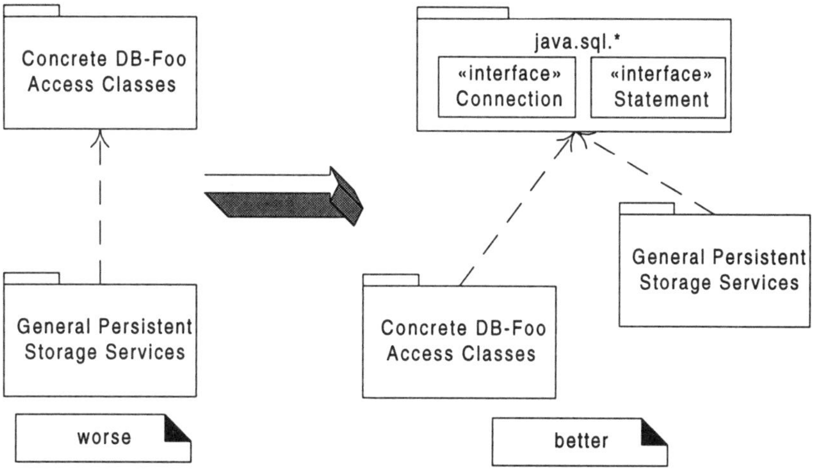

Observe that this guideline involves not only reorganizing types and packages, but also introducing new abstractions.

Exceptions to the Rule

This is not a hard-and-fast rule. For example, many packages rely on very concrete JDK packages such as *java.lang*. In addition, we sometimes create our own utility packages of fairly low-level services that are widely depended upon—even by more abstract packages. The key point motivating this guideline is that in general concrete packages tend to be less stable than abstract packages and so designing abstractions that depend on more concrete elements can increase the overall fragility of the design. However, if one is confident that a concrete package is very stable (such as *java.lang* or some simple utility package) then it is reasonable to ignore this guideline.

This is also known as the **Dependency Inversion Principle** [Martin 1995].

Guideline: Change Affects All or Nothing in a Package

Organize types into packages so that when a *predictable* change occurs in the future, most or all of the types are impacted in a package, or none are impacted: all or nothing.

One aspect of this guideline is to organize packages to isolate future changes in one or a few packages. This will reduce change propagation across packages, which decreases the cost and complexity of modification.

A second aspect is to "concentrate" packages so that a predictable change affects most of the types in the package. For example, suppose a package has fifty types, and is also quite *responsible*. Furthermore, assume that only a subset of ten of those types are going to experience likely change. By leaving the small subset of less stable types in the larger package, the larger package, which has many dependents, becomes less stable.

Alternatively the small subset can be factored into its own package. Then the predicted change will affect all or most of the types in the package: all or nothing.

Identifying these predictable changes, and designing "flex points" for them in software architecture, is a significant part of the art of a software architect.

For example, suppose security is one aspect of a financial instruments trading system, but in version 1.0, it is very lightweight. We perceive—through product plans, customer and market forces, and so on—that improving the security based on roles and access control lists will be a future area of change/improvement in the software. If the current lightweight role-based aspects of the security subsystem are bundled into the overall *Security* package, but just the role-based aspects are most likely to change in the future, then it would be desirable to factor those aspects into a separate package, as illustrated in Figure 12.4.

Figure 12.4 Redesign to support all-or-nothing future change impact.

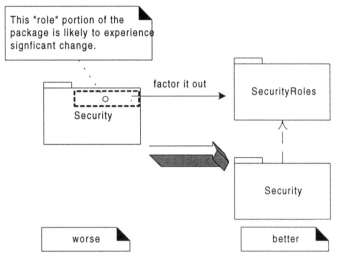

This guideline may be viewed as a corollary of a fundamental principle of object-oriented design first codified by the object technology pioneer Betrand Meyer: the **Open-Closed Principle** [Meyer 1988], and the idea of **common closure** with respect to a particular category of change. It may also be viewed as a realization of **high cohesion**.

GUIDELINE: FACTOR OUT INDEPENDENT TYPES

> Organize types that can be used independently or in different contexts into separate packages.

Without careful consideration, grouping by common function may not provide the right level of granularity in the factoring of packages.

For example, suppose that a subsystem for persistence services has been defined in one package *com.icbm.service.persistence*. In this package are two very general utility/helper classes *JDBCUtililities* and *SQLCommand*. If these are general utilities for working with JDBC, then they can be used independently of the persistence subsystem, for any occasion when the developer is using JDBC. Therefore, it is better to migrate these types into a separate package, such as *com.icbm.util.jdbc*. Figure 12.5 illustrates this.

Figure 12.5 Factoring out independent types.

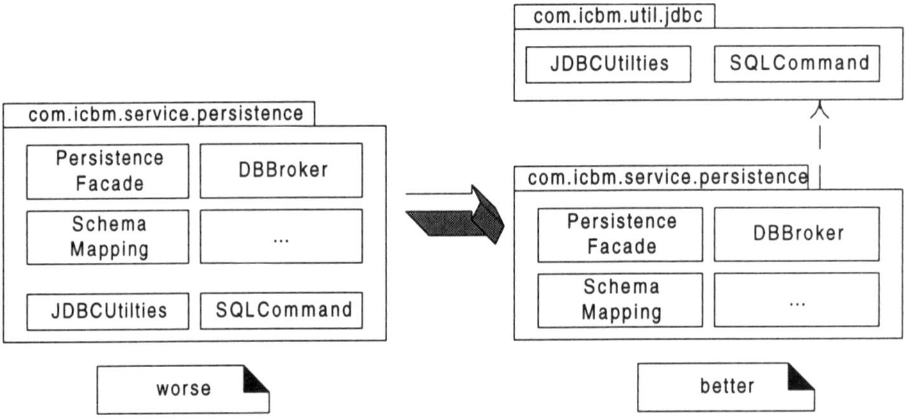

GUIDELINE: USE FACTORIES TO REDUCE DEPENDENCY ON CONCRETE PACKAGES

If we wish to support the principle of *don't depend on more concrete packages,* or otherwise reduce our dependency on concrete classes in other packages, then a combination of adding interfaces and a **factory object** can help.

Figure 12.6 and Figure 12.7 illustrate this. Suppose that classes *X* and *Y* create instances of *A, B,* and *C* from another concrete package. We can reduce the coupling to this concrete package by using a *factory object* that creates the instances, but whose *create* methods return objects declared in terms of interfaces rather than classes. In addition, the factory object can be designed as a meta-data factory, that does uses *java.lang.reflect.Constructor* objects to create instances; this decouples the factory from the concrete implementation package as well. The idiom using *Constructor* objects to create other objects is described in the chapter on library idioms using reflection.

Factory objects are used in the Enterprise JavaBeans (EJB) architecture. The EJB *Home* object plays the role of the factory object, and returns references declared as interfaces.

The reduced coupling to a concrete package comes at the expense of increased complexity in the design, so the application of this guideline should be applied sparingly—when flexibility and low coupling with respect to creation are critical.

Figure 12.6 Direct coupling to concrete package due to creation.

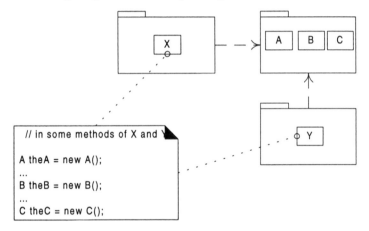

Figure 12.7 Reduced coupling to a concrete package by using a factory object.

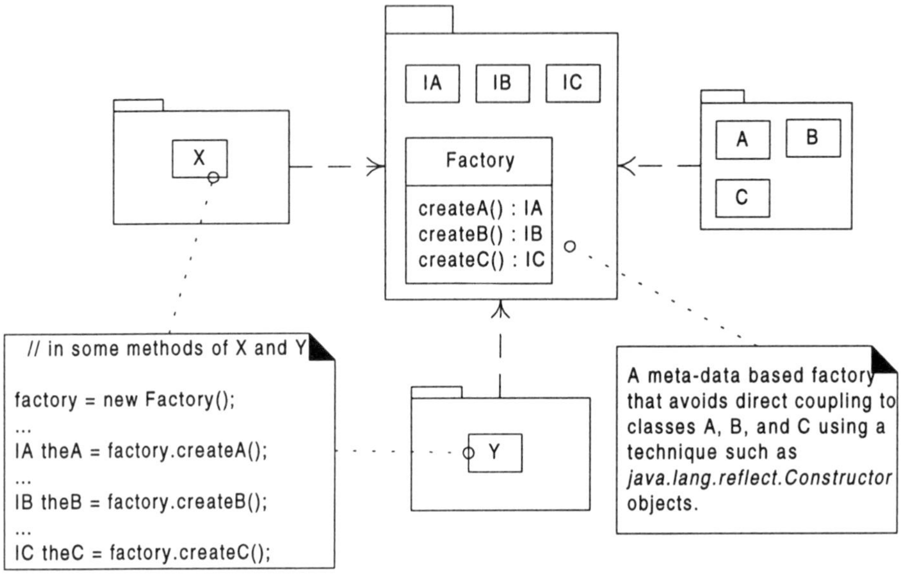

```
// in some methods of X and Y

factory = new Factory();
...
IA theA = factory.createA();
...
IB theB = factory.createB();
...
IC theC = factory.createC();
```

A meta-data based factory that avoids direct coupling to classes A, B, and C using a technique such as *java.lang.reflect.Constructor* objects.

GUIDELINE: NO CYCLES IN PACKAGES

Organize types in packages so that there are no cyclic dependencies.

If a group of packages have cyclic dependency then they may need to be treated as one larger package in terms of a release unit. This is not desirable.

One strategy to correct this is to factor out the types participating in the cycle into a new separate package. Another strategy is to break the cycle by the following steps. This example will assume that classes in separate packages depended on each other.

1. Redefine the depended-on classes in one of the packages to implement new interfaces.

2. Define the new interfaces in a new package.

3. Redefine the dependent types to depend on the interfaces in the new package, rather than the original classes.

Figure 12.8 illustrates this strategy.

Figure 12.8 Breaking a cyclic dependency.

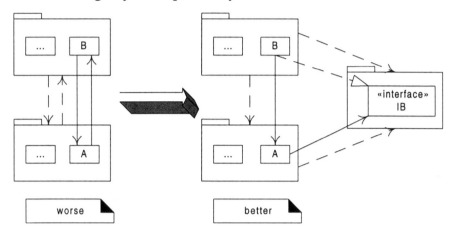

13 TESTING IDIOMS

In this chapter

- Idioms of class-level unit testing for faults.
- Suggested process changes to increase actual testing.

This chapter introduces some common idioms that Java developers use to unit test classes, and some Java-specific unit testing advice, because this is a development task normally performed by the class programmer, rather than a separate testing team.

There are several varieties of testing: fault (or correctness) testing, load testing, usability testing, unit testing, scenario testing, and so on. The chapter focuses on the foundation of object-oriented testing: unit-level fault testing of Java classes.

THE GOAL: INCREASED QUALITY

Testing is a means to an end: increased quality in the software product, such as reduced defects and increased reliability. To that end, in addition to examining the common practice of object-oriented unit testing, at the end of this chapter we consider a few closely related processes to encourage developers to actually *write* the tests, and produce higher quality.

13.1 WHITE-BOX TESTING WITH JAVA 2 REFLECTION

Before we get into a larger example of testing, it is worth noting that a new feature in the Java 2 Reflection API allows us to more easily perform white-box testing. We will create a helper class based on this feature.

White-box testing is based on knowledge of the internals of a component—typically a Java class. This can include evaluating the private instance fields and hidden structural representations. An example of white-box testing is to write test code that looks at a private field value of an object that you just modified, and test that the value is as expected. This of course turns out to be useful when there is no public accessing method for a field.

In contrast, black-box testing is based on only exercising the public interface of a component. Tests are written without knowledge of or dependency on the internals of the component. Both forms of testing are worthwhile. White-box tests are usually only written by the class developer.

In Java 2, the *java.lang.reflect.** member types (*Field*, *Method*, and *Constructor*) inherit from a new superclass: *AccessibleObject*.

The types inherit the new method *setAccessible(boolean)* which, if set to *true*, suppresses the default access control of members, so that it is possible to access private fields of other objects.

The following simplified class *FieldAccessor* provides a static service *get* to do this, which we will use in later examples. The complete version includes accessor methods for primitive types, such as *getInt*. See Listing 13.1.

Listing 13.1 A FieldAccessor that uses Java 2 Reflection capabilities.

```
import java.lang.reflect.*;

public final class FieldAccessor
{

  /**
   * Return the value of the field fieldName for obj
   * using Java 2 Reflection with suppressed access control.
   */
  public static Object get( Object obj, String fieldName )
  {
    try
    {
      Field field = obj.getClass().getDeclaredField( fieldName );
      field.setAccessible( true );        // the key step!
      return field.get( obj );
    }
    catch( Exception ex )
    {
      ex.printStackTrace();
      throw new RuntimeException( "Failed field access" );
    }
  }
}
```

13.2 UNIT TESTING EXAMPLE: APPLYING A JAVA TESTING FRAMEWORK—JUNIT

A **testing framework** is a set of types (in Java) that at the very least provide services for setting up and running test cases and suites for unit testing.

Unit testing refers to testing a discrete software component. In object technology, a *class* is a typical unit of testing. A suite of fault tests is written that exercises the behavior of a single class. A **test case** is simply one test. In the context of unit testing, it may refer to a test of one behavior, such as the *equals* method, or a group of related behaviors, such as a test case for all the methods that cause output to streams. A **test suite** is a set of test cases that are run as a group. In pattern terminology, a test suite is a *CompositeTestCase*.

A testing framework is the most popular kind of object-oriented testing tool. Frequently, an organization will craft their own testing framework, or start from a public domain one, and customize it. In this section we examine a *sample* testing framework and its idiomatic use.

JUnit is a simple, useful, free, open-source Java testing framework—and relatively popular in the Java community—implemented by Kent Beck and Erich Gamma. It was primarily designed by Beck as the Java variant of his original Smalltalk testing framework **SUnit** (there is also a C++ variant named **CppUnit**). It is available from the website www.armaties.com.

Although JUnit is a possible starting point for the creation of your own testing tool, the objective of this section is not to illustrate JUnit per se, but rather to demonstrate common responsibilities in and basic usage of a unit testing framework. On top of the basics of JUnit, there are several enhancements for a production testing framework that you will want to make; these are covered in a later section.

DEFINING A TEST CASE

JUnit includes an abstract superclass *test.framework.TestCase* from which new test cases can be derived. For example, to test the class *Sale*, we can define the class *TestCaseSale* as a subclass of *TestCase*. The listings for the *Sale* class and its associated members are found at the end of this chapter.

Listing 13.2 Test cases extend *test.framework.TestCase* in JUnit.

```
package sample.testing;

import test.framework.*;
```

```
import java.util.*;

public final class TestCaseSale extends TestCase
{
    // ...
}
```

The first test case to write is one that tests a *typical usage* of the class. This is implemented as a method in the test case class. Note that there is an inherited *assert* method that is used to perform the test. Tests that fail in the *assert* method are recorded by the framework for subsequent reporting.

Listing 13.3 shows the *testAddSaleLineItem* method. Observe the use of the *FieldAccessor* class to access a private field, and the use of the *assert* method to perform the tests. This method exhaustively tests that all expected state changes are true.

Listing 13.3 A "typical usage" test case method.

```
public void testAddSaleLineItem()
{
    // the typical usage is to add a new SaleLineItem to a Sale

    Sale s = new Sale();
    s.addNewSaleLineItemFor(For( 2, product1 );

    // note use of private field accessing using Java 2 features

    List lineItems = (List) FieldAccessor.get( s, "lineItems" );

    // there should be 1 member, of type SaleLineItem

    assert( lineItems.size() == 1 );
    assert( lineItems.get( 0 ) instanceof SaleLineItem );

    SaleLineItem sli = (SaleLineItem) lineItems.get( 0 );

    // its quantity should be 2, its product == product1

    assert( sli.getQuantity() == 2 );
    assert( sli.getProduct() == product1 );
}
```

In addition to a typical usage test, another common test is that initialization is correct. This is illustrated in Listing 13.4.

Listing 13.4 Testing initialization

```
public void testInitialization()
{
    // typical initialization

  Sale s = new Sale();

  List lineItems = (List) FieldAccessor.get( s, "lineItems" );

  assert( lineItems.size() == 0 );
  assert( s.getTotal() == 0 );

    // test that the date is today

  Calendar time = Calendar.getInstance();
  time.setTime( s.getDate() );
  Calendar saleTime = Calendar.getInstance();

  assert( time.get( Calendar.DAY_OF_YEAR ) ==
          saleTime.get( Calendar.DAY_OF_YEAR ) );
}
```

DEFINING A TEST SUITE

Now that we have defined two test case methods, we would like to run them together in a test suite. JUnit requires that we add a static method named *suite* that creates and returns a *test.framework.TestSuite* object (which implements the interface *Test*).

The *TestCase* class includes a constructor that takes the name of a testing method as a parameter. Listing 13.5 illustrates the appropriate methods in *TestCaseSale*.

Listing 13.5 A test suite method in *TestCaseSale*.

```
public TestCaseSale( String methodName )
{
  super( methodName );
}


public static Test suite()
```

```
{
  TestSuite suite = new TestSuite();
  suite.addTest( new TestCaseSale( "testAddSaleLineItem" ) );
  suite.addTest( new TestCaseSale( "testInitialization" ) );
  return suite;
}
```

RUNNING A TEST SUITE

JUnit includes both a command line driver and a Java GUI driver to run a test suite. It executes the set of test cases, and reports *assert* failures in a list box.

Listing 13.6 JUnit TestRunner.

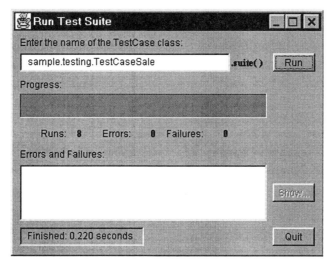

DEFINING AND USING TEST FIXTURES

A **fixture** or **test fixture** is the set of properly initialized objects against which a test runs. Subclasses of *TestCase* may define instance fields and a *setUp* method to create a test fixture. Listing 13.7 illustrates the *TestCaseSale* example. Setting up the fixture often consumes more effort than testing the fixture values.

A testing method does not have to use a predefined fixture implemented as instance fields. Sometimes it is most appropriate to set up and use local variable values.

Listing 13.7 `Setting up a test fixture.`

```
public final class TestCaseSale extends TestCase
{
    // test fixture variables

    private Sale                 sale1 = new Sale();
    private Sale                 sale2 = new Sale();
    private Sale                 sale3 = new Sale();
    private ProductDescription   product1 =
        new ProductDescription( 5, "p1" );
    private ProductDescription   product2 =
        new ProductDescription( 10, "p2" );



    /**
     * Set up the test fixture.
     */
    protected void setUp()
    {
        sale1.addNewSaleLineItemFor( 2, product1 );
        sale1.addNewSaleLineItemFor( 2, product1 );

        sale2.addNewSaleLineItemFor( 2, product1 );
        sale2.addNewSaleLineItemFor( 2, product1 );

        sale3.addNewSaleLineItemFor( 3, product2 );
        sale3.addNewSaleLineItemFor( 3, product2 );
    }
```

Once defined, the test case methods may exercise the fixture, as in the *testEquality* method shown next.

```
public void testEquality()
{
    assert( sale1.equals( sale1 ) );
    assert( sale1.equals( sale2 ) );
    assert( !sale1.equals( sale3 ) );
}
```

13.3 The Order of Unit Testing

It is a Good Thing to both implement and unit test your least coupled classes first. Start from the "leaf" classes and work inward to the most coupled classes—in other words, *bottom up* implementation and testing. Listing 13.8 illustrates an example order. For example, since *TaxingRegion* and *ProductDescription* have no dependencies, either could be implemented and unit tested first.

It is important that the unit test for a class be written, and the class debugged, before moving on to higher level classes. This ensures that as we build the more dependent classes, the components they depend on can be confidently relied upon to work.

Listing 13.8 Implementation and unit testing order.

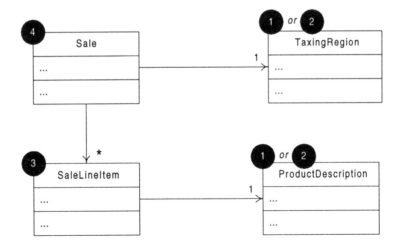

TESTING FRAMEWORK ENHANCEMENTS

JUnit is a simple testing framework, and this example has emphasized the basics. Many enhancements are desirable for a larger-scale framework. These include:

- Add or remove test cases and suites by the addition or removal of Java testing class files from special testing directories. The main testing driver will dynamically organize the set of tests by loading all class files in the testing directories. This approach has the advantage of not requiring source code modification and recompilation of the test suite definitions.

- User-specified output stream for test failure results, such as to a particular file.

- Define test run properties using a "properties" file. These could include the name of a results files, the names of test case methods to run, verbosity of error messages, number of repetitions of the test suite, and so forth.

13.4 REGRESSION TESTING

Regression testing refers to testing to ensure that the product has not *regressed* to a worse state after changes have been made. A previously successful test suite is run against the product after change to help determine if defects have crept in. A key requirement in regression testing is to *not* remove any of the old tests as the system evolves (unless they are no longer valid), although it is acceptable to add new tests. In Java, each time a class is modified, the test suite that was used to previously validate the class should be run again.

13.5 WHAT TO TEST—AND NOT TEST

A few guiding principles can be stated about the tests to write:

- Test methods which cause change of state (change in instance fields), except for simple *set* methods, which are usually trivial and reliable. This includes methods which cause the forming and breaking of associations with other objects, the creation of objects, the acquisition of resources, and so on.

- Test boundary conditions and high load conditions.

- Test expected failures. Suppose your new Java text editor should be able to save files to the hard disk but the disk (or partition) is full. Better to test the outcome beforehand than have a customer "explain" what happened.

In contrast to the above, there are some things *not* worth testing:

- When writing a unit test for class *A*, don't test the internal state of objects pointed to by *A*—assume they are correct. This follows from the order of implementation and testing: bottom up. By the time we create and test *A*, the classes that *A* is dependent upon should already have been testing and debugged.

- Don't bother testing the correctness of simple accessing methods, such as Java-Beans *get* and *set* methods. One reason is that most IDEs contain wizard tools that automatically generate the *get* and *set* methods, so it is unnecessary to test them—they work. And even if hand-generated (which is a bad idea if you've got an IDE that can do it), these methods are almost never faulty. Writing these method tests is laborious and rarely produces a failure.

13.6 JAVA-SPECIFIC TESTING ADVICE

PLACE TESTING CODE IN A DIFFERENT PACKAGE

Do not define testing classes within the same package as the code to be tested. This is because it complicates the configuration of a production system—in which the testing classes should be *excluded*. In most IDEs, it would require a manual selection of a subset of classes from each package, rather than the entire package, to include in the production system (for example, in a JAR file). Such handcrafting is not a tenable practice in configuration management.

Name Testing Package Names Starting with "test"

When configuring a Java production system, some IDEs support the creation of a production JAR file by selecting packages from a graphical list box that displays all package names, alphabetically sorted. Consider having to select the non-testing packages from the following list:

```
com.objectspace.foo.a
com.objectspace.foo.a.test
com.objectspace.foo.b
com.objectspace.foo.b.test
com.objectspace.foo.c
com.objectspace.foo.c.test
```

The obvious defect is that the testing packages are interleaved with the production packages, because of the naming convention chosen for the testing packages. This complicates the manual step of choosing the production packages. In contrast, consider:

```
com.objectspace.foo.a
com.objectspace.foo.b
com.objectspace.foo.c
test.com.objectspace.foo.a
test.com.objectspace.foo.b
test.com.objectspace.foo.c
```

The testing packages sort together, and are easy to identify and ignore when choosing production packages for a JAR file. Therefore, consider naming testing packages starting with "test."

No Testing Methods in the Class to Be Tested

The previous advice to place testing code in a different package of course implies that testing code should not be in the *class* to be tested, either. Grouping testing code into the tested class *is* possible in fully compiled languages in which the compiler and linker will ensure that unnecessary code is not included in the final executable. However, in Java the production class file will contain the bytecode for *all* methods, including testing method (unless a special bytecode optimizer is applied). This needlessly increases the class file size with non-production code (and adds visual clutter).

Design for a Configurable PrintStream

It is desirable to be able to redirect the testing output to an arbitrary *PrintStream*, such as to *System.out*, or to a file. Therefore, design a testing framework to support this. For example, *Tester.out* can be defined as the standard output stream for results:

```
Tester.out.println( … );
```

Specify the specific output stream in a "testing properties" file that the framework reads from during initialization.

13.7 "HUMAN-NATURE BASED" TESTING

Learning how write a unit test is not of much value if it doesn't get done! Perhaps in no other area of software engineering is there a more lopsided ratio of advice to practice than the field of testing. We think this is due to inattention to the psychological and social aspects of testing.

Thinking about and writing tests is relatively uninteresting—that's the plain truth. Breaking away from programming to work with a fussy testing tool is disruptive and unpleasant. Some testing methods are too formal, complex, or laborious for the patience of the average software engineer. People—even programmers—take the path of least resistance. A workable testing approach for non-mission-critical software needs to use *simple* tools, techniques, and testing processes.

Exception: An important exception to this suggestion is mission-critical or life-threatening software, such as avionics controls. In those domains, exhaustive, rigorous formal testing and a highly structured testing organization are necessary ingredients in achieving the high level of reliability that is demanded of such products.

Any recommended system or practice that does not consider human nature, be it Communism or an unwieldy testing regimen, is doomed to failure. Consequently, we offer some "human-nature based" guidelines to practically increase the likelihood that useful testing will actually get done.

Developers Design the Unit Testing Strategy

At the start of a project, establish developer commitment to a testing regimen by organizing a "testing" meeting where the developers themselves decide upon the plan and tools. Afterwards, the project and technical leads need to follow through by regularly paying attention to testing issues, and the testing regimen decided upon by the developers.

Integrate Unit Testing into Development

This is very important. Writing and executing unit tests (for Java classes) must become an integral part of the rhythm of programming, not an afterthought that occurs after a week (or worse, six months!) of heads-down programming. As each class is developed, the class developer should write the unit test for it; some even recommend writing simple unit tests *before* the class to be tested. It is the class developer who has the deepest insight into the class, and if the unit test is written around the same time as the class, the developer has a fresh memory of the details of the class, and what is worth testing.

Separate Testers Perform Scenario Testing

Although unit tests are most practically written and executed by the class developer, scenario testing[1] (testing the major scenarios of interacting with and using a system or subsystem) of the entire application (or its subsystems) should be done by separate test personnel. The developers are likely to engage in wishful thinking (or more likely, exhaustion!) and unconsciously or consciously avoid performing the hard (or "dumb") tests that can break the system. A separate testing team comes to the testing task with more vigor and less familiarity, which is essential to tease out the defects.

---

1. Also known as use-case based testing.

DON'T FORGET CODE INSPECTIONS AND DESIGN REVIEWS

Consider the following true story about a software system contracted by the U.S. Air Force:

- The contractors estimated two years for development, but the Air Force insisted it be done in one year.

- The software had to be developed on a different workstation brand than the delivery workstation (because of production delays), and then ported.

- The NORAD users wanted ten times the original functions specified in the requirements.

An obvious software disaster, right? Wrong. The system was completed on time and budget. In the following months of production use, users found only two bugs.

The secret to its success was that the team leader promoted a major campaign of *code inspections and design reviews* by the team members.

Years ago, the software productivity expert Capers Jones illustrated that code inspection and design review is significantly more effective in reducing defects than software testing [Jones 1981]. Yet this valuable advice is still all-too-seldom put into practice.

Here are some suggestions to increase the likelihood that inspection/review will occur:

- *Programming in Pairs* is the ideal mechanism to achieve inspection/review. The review occurs while the code is being written. The observer has the best insight and is mentally engaged—mindful of the design, context, and details related to the code.

- Run design review and code inspection meetings separately. It may be difficult to get commitment to or engagement in code inspection meetings—which are laborious and detailed. However, most software engineers are relatively inter-ested in—and enjoy—design review meetings.

- Do not expect any pre-meeting inspection of your code or design documents; for example, via prior distribution of a program listing. Do the work in the meeting. Most people are too busy, uninterested, or lack the necessary feedback to do a proper evaluation on their own. No matter what the testing-experts tell you about proper pre-meeting preparation, *it ain't gonna happen*.

- Establish inspection or review meetings at a weekly, consistent time in order to establish a habit.

- Reviewers need to be mindful to avoid blaming team members, so that every-one feels comfortable in the process.

INCLUDE TESTING CODE INSPECTIONS DURING REVIEWS

During the regular code inspection meetings, include inspection of the *testing code*. This will elevate the importance and ongoing commitment to creating tests during the development process; ignoring them during reviews gives the unfortunate mes-sage that the tests are not of consequence.

BEWARE TESTING FRAMEWORK-ITIS

Since building frameworks is fun, writing test code is mundane, software develop-ers are creative, and most people procrastinate, a common disease on a project is to spend more time fiddling with polishing up, generalizing, and enhancing the test-ing framework, than with *using* the testing framework to write real tests. We call this **framework-itis**.

14 CODING IDIOMS—NAMING

In this chapter

■ Common practices when naming elements in Java.

A colleague of ours used to joke that he wished he could hire a sidekick who had the ability to choose *the* name, the perfect name, at the snap of his fingers. Oh, if it were only that easy! Instead, our colleague continues to labor over the right name, the name that is concise, precise, and clear in meaning. Naming idioms, while not as good as our fictional sidekick, can improve the way we choose names because in many cases, they remove the choice altogether. In other cases, they lead us in the right direction.

There are eight types of names in Java. They are (in order of granularity) package, class or interface, field, method, parameter, and local variable names [GJS 1996]. There are guidelines for choosing names of each type.

Regardless of the name being chosen, the issue of name length will arise. There are two competing forces in this decision. The name should be concise, but it should also be precise. Unfortunately, *concise* pulls names to the short side while *precise* pulls names to the long side. As Kent Beck, one of the fathers of OOP, says, optimize the naming scheme for reading (a 1000 to 10,000-time occurrence in 20 years) over typing (a 10 to 100-time occurrence over 20 years). That is, the extra typing will pay off over the next few thousand reads [Beck 1997].

A special note has to be made regarding code generation. Many modern development environments generate boiler-plate code for fields, methods, and in some cases even classes. This is particularly the case in the realm of JavaBeans, and GUIs. Do not attempt to post-process this code to fit the naming recommendations presented here. This will only complicate things. Let the code generator do its thing.

14.1 IDIOMS FOR PACKAGE NAMES

Java programs are typically organized into one or more **packages**. A package provides four features for Java developers.

1. It provides a scope for access protection.
2. It helps reduce change impact when releasing.
3. It allows classes to be grouped for high-level functional cohesion.
4. It provides a name space that helps prevent name clashes.

Developers should package classes using the standard Java package naming convention [GJS 1996]. This convention has five very simple rules:

> Package names are dot-delimited as in *a.b.c.SomeClass*. In this example, *b* is a subpackage of *a*, and *c* is a subpackage of *b*. Subpackages allow for hierarchical organization of packages.
>
> Package names must not begin with the identifier *java*. These package names are reserved for Sun Microsystems for use in packaging core Java classes.

Package names should begin with a lower case letter. This prevents the possibility of mistaking a package name for a class name (which, by convention, should begin with an upper case letter). In fact, package names should usually consist entirely of lower case letters.

Package names should be meaningful in the context for which the code is being written. For example, packaged an *Entry* class might be placed in a package called *orderentry* because this package name has meaning for an order entry system.

Package names should be prefixed with a two or three letter Internet domain code—or two-letter ISO country code—applicable to the organization developing the software. It should also include the name of the organization

The following package names are typical of names chosen under this convention:

```
com.objectspace.voyager
gov.sandia.mdl.images
edu.uiuc.cave
be.ac.rug.templates
```

Beyond these simple rules, package naming becomes less important than the actual structure of the packages being created. This topic is covered in the chapter on package organization

14.2 Idioms for Class and Interface Names

As with most things, there are two considerations for class and interface names: the content and the presentation. *The Java Language Specification* encourages a simple and easy to use formula [GSJ 1996]:

> Name classes and interfaces with descriptive nouns or noun phrases. Nouns are used because classes model things.

> Begin class and interface names with an uppercase letter and use mixed case for compound names. This style helps prevent name clashes with package and field names.

Beyond this there are a few idioms to consider when choosing the content for the names.

Subclass Names

All Java classes are subclasses because they either extend *Object* or they extend some other class. In the context of names, however, classes that extend *Object* are often named using a different set of rules than classes that do not directly extend *Object*. The reason is that names for classes that do not directly extend *Object* often need to convey two extra pieces of information: how the subclass is like the superclass and how the subclass differs from the superclass [Beck 1997]. Take, for example, a superclass named *Connection*. Suppose we want to extend this class with an implementation that provides authentication and data encryption. We might name the class *SecureConnection* to communicate that the class is a connection (how it is like *Connection*) but that it is in fact secure (how it differs from *Connection*).

Communicate how a subclass differs from its superclass in the subclass name.

This naming idiom should not always be applied, and choosing when to apply it is not always obvious. A general rule is that the name of the superclass should be incorporated into the name of the subclass when the concept modeled by the superclass is essential to the nature of the subclass.

Incorporate the superclass name into the subclass name when the concept modeled by the superclass is essential to the nature of the subclass.

This holds for interfaces as well. Interface names should be incorporated into the implementing class name when the concept modeled by the interface is essential to the class. For example, the *java.lang.reflect.Method* class does not implement *java.io.Serializable*. If we wanted to create a class that represented a method that could be serialized, we might call it a *SerializableMethod*. We incorporate *Serializable* into the name because the fact that the object can be serialized is the only reason for its existence. On the other hand, *java.util.ArrayList* implements *Serializable* but does not contain the word serializable in its name. The essential nature of an *ArrayList* is that it is a container for other objects. The fact that it can be marshaled to bytes is ancillary.

INTERFACE AND ABSTRACT CLASS NAMES

Interfaces exist in one form or another in several programming languages and component models. There are currently two competing idioms for naming interfaces: *to I or not to I*. That is, one convention—championed by Microsoft—holds that interface names begin with the letter I. The other convention—found in the Java packages—omits the I prefix. For example, the alternatives for naming an interface that represents the concept of an employee are *IEmployee* and *Employee*.

Many developers are moving to the I-convention because it instantly communicates the fact that the code construct is an interface. This is important because interfaces are the preferred way of specifying APIs and abstractions. Because of this, we recommend beginning interface names with *I* as in *IEmployee*, *IServer*, and *IConnection*[1].

> Prefix interface names with the letter "I".

Many times interfaces are used to convey the fact that a specific action can be performed on an object. For instance, the *java.lang.Comparable* interface is implemented by classes whose objects can be compared. These interface names often use the action name (or some significant part of the name) as the root, and end in *–able*. Examples from the Java class library include *Runnable* (with the *run* method), and *Cloneable* (with the *clone* method). This style of naming can be combined with the I-convention to form interface names like *ISendable*, and *IRecoverable*. (Note that these words are, strictly speaking, adjectives, not nouns. This is one of the few cases where type names are not chosen as nouns.)

> Append the *–able* suffix when naming interfaces that represent types on which one operation is possible.

---

1. We know, however, that these are issues on which reasonable people can disagree. As always, choose your standard and stick with it.

Abstract classes, like interfaces, are frequently used in APIs and frameworks. These classes are made instantly recognizable by using the *Abstract<x>* form. Most Java 2 abstract classes (for example *AbstractAction*, *AbstractButton*, and *AbstractCollection*) follow this style.

> Use the *Abstract<x>* form to name abstract classes.

EXCEPTION CLASS NAMES

Exceptions play a critical role in Java. They are the preferred way of indicating error conditions. The exception classes will need to be studied to understand the error handling subsystem of an application. On the other hand, if one is trying to understand overall structure of an application, exception classes are often in the way. It is rarely the case that an understanding of the structure of a system requires a thorough understanding of the exception classes and their relationships. Both of these points argue in favor of having a naming convention that readily identifies exception classes.

Exception classes are universally named using an *<x>Exception* form. This instantly conveys critical information about the nature of the class. By tagging the class as an exception, readers are able to ignore or focus on the class as needed.

> Name exception classes should be named using the *<x>Exception* form.

```
public class InvalidWithdrawalException extends Exception
```

ILLUSTRATING PATTERN USAGE

Design patterns help software developers apply well-known solutions to common problems. One way to make the nature of such system clear is to illustrate the usage of these design patterns by naming the participating classes after the pattern. For example, a *RemoteProxy* is instantly recognizable as a participant in the *Proxy* pattern [GHJV 1995]. Likewise, an *ActiveState* is obviously a participant in *State*, and *ConnectionFactory* is a participant in *Factory*.

> If a class is a major participant in a well-known design pattern, name the class after that pattern.

MAIN CLASSES

The *main(String[])* method is the entry point for any application run directly by a Java VM. These methods usually do little except kick off the application and, possibly, some error handling. It is common practice to factor these methods out of the application and into a special class that contains only the *main* method. This encourages a separation of concerns—functional cohesion. We recommend they be named *Main* for instant recognition. In applications that have multiple main programs, consider using *Main* as a suffix, as in *ClientMain* and *ServerMain*.

> Name main classes *Main* or *<x>Main*.

(See the library idioms chapter on exceptions for a version of *Main* that is designed to catch all unexpected exceptions. Consider using this as the canonical implementation of *Main*.)

14.3 Idioms for Field Names

Static final fields of interfaces (and less frequently classes) play the role of **constants** in Java. Constants and non-constants are written according to different standards. This promotes instant recognition and thus instantly communicates important information to the reader. In either case, field names, like class and interface names, should usually be nouns or noun phrases. For instance, *runner* might make a good field name, but *run* almost certainly would not.

Naming Non-Constant Fields

Names for fields that are not constant are written according to the following simple rule:

> Non-constant field names should begin with a lower case letter. If the name is a phrase, each word in the phrase except for the first begins with an upper case letter.

```
private static ClassLoader currentLoader;
private static int numberOfEmployees;

private String name;
private int age;
```

Naming Constant Fields

Abbreviations and acronyms are generally avoided in names. They do not convey information well and are often difficult to read. This rule is relaxed in the case of constants. Constant names should not be terse, but acceptable abbreviations are often available. For instance, the constants that represent the transaction modes of an Enterprise JavaBean component or method are

```
public static final int TX_BEAN_MANAGED   = 1
public static final int TX_MANDATORY      = 2
public static final int TX_NOT_SUPPORTED  = 3
public static final int TX_REQUIRED       = 4
public static final int TX_REQUIRES_NEW   = 5
public static final int TX_SUPPORTS       = 6
```

Constants often come in sets, as in this example, where each constant represents a different value in the set. In this case, the abbreviation *TX* is natural and well understood to mean *transaction*. As in this, constants should be written in upper case letters and underscore characters should separate individual words.

Write constant names in upper case letters and separate individual words with underscores.

```
public static final int MAX_SESSIONS = 10;
public static final String CONNECT_ERROR = "Unable to connect to server.";
```

FIELD NAMES FOR QUANTITIES

Quantities are so frequently encountered that standard names have emerged. Counters (fields used in incrementation) and tallies (fields used to store totals) are often named by appending *Count* to the concept name. This instantly identifies the numeric nature of the variable to the reader. Maxima and minima are also frequently encountered. The abbreviated prefixes *max* and *min* suffice to convey their nature. The following rules will take some of the thinking out of the quantity-naming chore.

> Counters and tallies use the *<x>Count* style.

```
private int employeeCount;
private int connectionCount;
```

> Maxima and minima get the *max* and *min* prefix respectively.

```
public static final long MIN_VALUE = 0x8000000000000000L;
public static final long MAX_VALUE = 0x7fffffffffffffffL;
private static int maxConnections = 20;

private int minClients = 0;
```

DEFAULT VALUES

Default values are also frequently encountered. This may come as a surprise, but we recommend the prefix *default* for all such values.

> Default values follow the *default<x>* style.

```
public static final int DEFAULT_PORT = 80;
private static String defaultName = "Unnamed Object";
```

BOOLEAN FIELDS

boolean fields (indeed all *boolean* variables) are almost exclusively named using the *is<X>* form. The reason is simple: *is<X>* asks a yes/no question. Is the stove on? Is a banana yellow? Booleans represent yes/no states. Perfect fit.

> Boolean fields follow the *is<X>* style.

```
private boolean isEnabled = false;
private boolean isLocked = true;
```

14.4 IDIOMS FOR METHOD NAMES

It is extremely important that good names are chosen for methods. In object-oriented languages like Java, method invocation often comprises the bulk of the code. In Java applications—indeed, in Java itself—most of the work will be done through delegation. This means that most of the effort in understanding what a piece of code means involves understanding what these methods do. Well-chosen names facilitate this.

Because methods represent actions or activities, they are usually named using verbs or verb phrases.

Use verbs or verb phrases to name methods.

```
public void run();
public void writeObject( ObjectOutputStream out ) throws IOException;
public boolean isEmpty()
```

The JavaBeans Method Naming Standard

The JavaBeans component model identifies several method naming conventions. These conventions allow for sophisticated **introspection** of a class. Introspection allows the introspecting party (for example, a GUI builder) to determine the nature of a class.

Under the JavaBeans model, all logical object properties should be accessed through property **getter** and **setter** methods (sometimes known as **accessors** and **mutators**). A getter method is a method that returns a property value. A setter is a method that modifies a property value. For example:

```
/**
 * Accessor method.
 */
public final String getName()
{
  return name;
}

/**
 * Mutator method
 */
public final void setName( String name )
{
  this.name = name;
}
```

Moreover, JavaBeans specifies a naming rule to make it easy to name these getters. There are two cases, based on whether or not the property is of type *boolean*. In either case, both getters and setters have public access protection. Getters have a return type of the same type as the property and take no arguments. Setters have a return type of void and accept a single argument of the same type as the property.

(Note that JavaBeans properties do not necessarily map down to fields. As such, the name of a field is completely unrelated to the name of the property. A *foo* field may be accessed through *getBar* and *setBar* methods. Keep this in mind when viewing IDE generated bean code. Some IDEs will use different names for the fields than for the properties.)

> Non-*boolean* JavaBeans properties should have a getter named by prefixing the name of the property with the word *get* and changing the first letter of the property name to upper case. For example, a property of type *int* named *age* should have a getter method named *getAge()* as in the following example.

```
public final int getAge()
{
   return age;
}
```

> *boolean* properties should have a getter named by prefixing the name of the property with the word *is* and changing the first letter of the property name to upper case. For example, a *boolean* property named *valid* should have a getter method named *isValid()* as in:

```
public final boolean isValid()
{
  return isValid;
}
```

> Both non-*boolean* and *boolean* properties should have a setter
> named by prefixing the name of the property with the word set
> and changing the first letter of the property name to upper case.
> For example, an *int* property named *age* should have a setter
> method name *setAge(int age)*.

```
public final void setAge( int age )
{
  this.age = age;
}
```

OTHER CONSISTENCY RULES FOR METHOD NAMES

There are rules to help name methods in addition to the JavaBeans consistency rules
for getters and setters. Many methods will fall into the one of the categories listed
below. Following the guidelines below will make it easier to choose names consistently.

> Methods that return boolean values should be prefixed with *is* if
> possible, *has* otherwise.

```
policy.isExpired();
policy.isValid();
person.isWithAutoPolicy(); // awkward, but maintains JavaBeans style
person.hasAutoPolicy(); // more natural, OK if not a Bean property
```

Methods that return an object and take a single parameter should use the *get<x>For* style unless there is a compelling alternative.

```
company.getPolicyFor( policyKey );
codeAnalyzer.getPackageNameFor( fullClassName );
```

Unless the methods access Beans properties, methods that return a collection or array should use the *getAll<x>* and *getAll<x>For* styles.

```
Collection vehicles = policy.getAllVehiclesBelow( maxYears );
Collection jarMetrics = codeAnalyzer.getAllJarMetricsFor( jarFileName );
Collection classes = codeAnalyzer.getAllNonSystemClassesFor( classes );
```

Factory methods (methods that create and return instances) should use the *create<x>* style. (This is consistent with the standard *create* methods of the factory objects in Enterprise JavaBeans, the so-called home interfaces.)

```
Policy policy = policyFactory.createPolicy();
Policy policy = policyFactory.createPolicyFor( key, date );
Collection newPolicies = policyFactory.createAllPolicies();
```

Methods that update or replace objects should use the *update<x>* or *update<x>For* style.

```
company.updatePolicy( policy );
company.updatePolicyFor( key, date );
```

Note that the subtle *company.update(policy)* form could have been used. This form, however, lacks proper identification of the object being updated. Though the parameter name may often contain this information, it may not always. Regardless, by omitting this information from the method name, we force the reader to look in two places to decipher the correct meaning of the method invocation. Again, all else being equal, clarity wins over brevity.

> Methods that add objects should use the *add<x>* style.

```
company.addPolicy( policy );
```

Again, *company.add(policy)* is a little too subtle. (On the other hand, the Collections API has *Collection.add*. This form was chosen for two reasons. First, unlike custom add methods, there is no type to encode in the method name and *addElement* or *addObject* would communicate nothing about the type that isn't patently obvious. Second, these methods are workhorses of the API so brevity is very desirable.)

> Methods that create and add objects should use the *addNew<x>* style.

```
businessRuleFactory.addNewRule();
businessRuleFactory.addAllNewRules(); // use the "All" for multiple addi-
tions
company.addNewPolicyFor( key );        // use the "For" with a parameter
```

> Methods that delete objects should use the *remove<x>* style.

```
company.removePolicy( policy );
company.removePolicyFor( key );
```

> Methods that convert use the *to<x>* style. (This form is used throughout the JDK.)

```
object.toString();     // see Object.toString
collection.toArray();  // see Collection.toArray
memento.toSerializedObject();
```

The validation method idiom, shown in the next example, involves using a void method that checks the value of a field or parameter. A valid value results in successful method completion while an invalid value results in an exception. Validation methods are often cleaner than boolean checks. Luckily, the names for these validation methods are also amenable to a consistency rule:

> Validation methods should use the *check<x>* style.

```
application.check();
application.checkAddress();
codeAnalyzer.checkNamingFor( classes );
```

For an example of validation methods in the JDK, see the *SecurityManager* class. The *check<x>* methods of this class are designed to complete successfully if the security check passes—and to fail with a *SecurityException* otherwise.

14.5 Idioms for Parameter and Local Variable Names

Formal Parameters (arguments to methods) and local variables are named in much the same way that fields are named. Like fields, parameters and local variables are given meaningful yet not overly long names, and they are written in mixed case. Unlike fields, however, there are several exceptions to the rule that, for better or worse, have become accepted Java style.

> Used lowercase nouns or mixed case noun phrases for parameters and local variables.

```
public void disconnectFrom( URL serverURL )
{
  Connection connection = getConnectionFor( serverURL );
  securityManager.checkDisconnect( connection );
  connection.disconnect();
}
```

Common Abbreviations for Local Variables

Name abbreviations have come in to widespread use for streams, loop indices, iterators, and exceptions. Most other abbreviations are to be avoided.

> Use *in* and *out* when streams are used for input and output.

```
FileInputStream in = new FileInputStream( filename );
System.out.println( "Notice the use of _out_ for the output field." );
DataInputStream in = new DataInputStream( socket.getInputStream() );
```

> Name loop counters *i*. If nesting loops, use the next available letter (j, k, l, and so forth).

```
for ( int i = 0; i < args.length; i++ )
  System.out.println( args[ i ] );

for ( int i = 0; i < args.length; i++ )
{
  String arg = args[ i ];

  for ( int j = 0; j < arg.length(); j++ )
    System.out.println( arg[ j ] );
}
```

> Abbreviate iterator names using the letter *i*. Note that this is another example of 100% adherence to a style because *for* loops on arrays also use the letter *i* as the loop index variable.

```
for ( Iterator i = services.iterator(); i.hasNext(); )
  ( (IService) i.next() ).startup();
```

> Abbreviate exception names using *ex*.

```
try
{
  message = in.readUTF();
}
catch ( IOException ex )
{
  throw new CommunicationException( "Unable to read message", ex );
}
```

For nested exception handlers, use a numeric qualifier or other simple qualification scheme.

```
try
{
  factory = Class.forName( args[ 0 ] );

  try
  {
    object = factory.newInstance();
    // ...
  }
  catch ( Exception ex2 )
  {
    // ...
  }
}
catch ( ClassNotFoundException ex )
{
  // ...
}
```

The last recommended abbreviation is the ever-present *args* parameter for *main* methods.

Use *args* to name the *String[]* parameter to *main* methods.

```
public static void main( String[] args )
{
  System.out.println( args.length );
}
```

Choosing Parameter Names for Field Initialization

There are multiple ways to name parameters that are used to set field values. Some programmers that came to Java from Smalltalk use article-prefixed type names for parameters as in:

```
// WORSE
public Employeee( String aString )
{
  name = aString;
}
```

As they become assimilated by the Java hordes, however, they tend to abandon this form.

Former C programmers often prefer underscore mangling as in:

```
// WORSE
public Employee( String name_ )
{
  name = name_;
}
```

This style is considered hard to read and hard to type by many, so its use is becoming rare.

Perhaps the most common form is the **scope-resolution** style. The scope-resolution style names the parameter the same as the field and uses the *this* keyword to resolve the meaning of the assignment as in:

```
// BETTER

public Employee( String name )
{
   this.name = name;
}
```

> When a parameter name is used to mutate or initialize a field, the name of the parameter is chosen to be the same as the name of the field and scope is resolved using the *this* keyword.

```
public final void setAge( int age )
{
   this.age = age;
}

public void initialize( Make make, Model model )
{
   this.make = make;
   this.model = model;
}
```

(One exception to this rule is when a field is caching a JavaBeans property. Because JavaBeans does not require properties to be named after fields in which they are cached, do not feel you have to name the field exactly like the property. Likewise, the initialization parameter does not have to be named the same as the field. Though it is often convenient to do so when creating the code manually, many IDEs will choose a different naming convention. Believe us, this is one case where you don't want to fight the power. Let them have their way.)

One unfortunate consequence of this standard is the possibility of errors due to accidental omissions of the *this* keyword and subtle typos. Because the compiler cannot catch them, they can only be found at runtime. For example, the following type could result in a *NullPointerException* or an incorrectly initialized field value.

```
// BUG!!!

/**
 * The compiler can't catch this one!  Note the two e's in the
 * parameter name.
 */
public final void setDescriptor( DeploymentDescriptor deescriptor )
{
   this.descriptor = descriptor; // sets the field to its current value
}

/**
 * But it can catch this one.
 */
public final void setDescriptor( DeploymentDescriptor deescriptor_ )
{
   this.descriptor = descriptor_; // descriptor_ has never been declared!
}
```

Likewise, forgetting the *this* keyword in the following example would probably result in a *NullPointerException* somewhere down the road:

```
/**
 * If a mangling style such as the underscore notation is used,
 * the following would never occur. These are more common in more
 * complex methods.
 */
public final void setDescriptor( DeploymentDescriptor descriptor )
{
   descriptor = descriptor; // sets the parameter to its current value
}
```

By this point you're probably wondering what masochist would choose the scope-resolution style. Luckily, in practice these bugs rarely occur, and when they do they are often obvious. The consensus in the Java community seems to be that the time spent thinking up a non-clashing name and the usual awkwardness of the result are worse than the possibility of one of the bugs mentioned here. The JDK makes frequent use of the scope-resolution style.

15 CODING IDIOMS—STYLE

In this chapter

- Some low-level coding idioms.

The techniques presented in this chapter are very low level style idioms that, over years of use, have been found to simplify code. Note that *Composed Method* and *Intention Revealing Message* are not Java specific, but are general style guidelines applicable to any object-oriented language (and in slightly modified form, to procedural languages as well). They are included here because of the degree to which they can improve code.

15.1 COMPOSED METHOD

Kent Beck summarizes the best practice advice for defining and factoring methods in his coding pattern **Composed Method** [Beck 1997].

- A method should have *one* clearly definable responsibility.

- The operations within the method should be at a similar level of abstraction. (This is often overlooked.)

- In general, a method should be "short" (such as visible within an editor pane).

Well-composed methods tend to be highly readable, and seldom require commenting within the body of the method.[1]

Most methods with significant responsibilities do not start out well composed. It is quite common to first write the method in a longer and less composed form in order to work out the logic. Then the method is refactored to improve its composition and readability.

In an ideal world, the factoring would be done with the help of a smart editor that we use by simply selecting a section of code to factor out into a helper method, and the editor would do all the work of defining the helper method and inserting a call to it. The inventive researchers and students at UIUC have developed such a wonderful "refactoring browser" for Smalltalk IDEs. However, there is not one yet available for Java.

Breaking a large method into smaller methods is pretty obvious. Less obvious is achieving a similar level of abstraction in the operations of the method. The following case study illustrates the thought process of factoring and "leveling" an increasingly better *Composed Method*.

Listing 15.1 An un-composed method.

```
// WORSE - not an ideal Composed Method

/**
 * Calculate the outgoing package coupling for a class.
 * Record the results in an updated network of Nodes that
 * is held by this object.
 *
 * @param    fileName    name of class file in the zipFile.
 * @param    zipFile     a zip file or jar containing class files.
```

---

1. This advice is more generally an aspect of **refactoring** code. A broader treatment of the subject, emphasizing Java, is presented in [Fowler 1999]. Some find the name "composed method" slightly curious. We have kept it out of a desire to avoid re-inventing names. It is meant to suggest "well-composed" or refined.

```
  */
private void calculateMetrics( String fileName, ZipFile zipFile )
{
    try
    {
      ClassFile file = loader.getClassFileFromZip( fileName, zipFile );
      Collection classes = getAllNonSystemClassesFor( file.getClasses() );
      Collection packages = getAllPackageNodesFor( classes );

❶    String tempName = fileName.replace( '/', '.' );
      String packageName = getPackageNameFor( tempName );

❷    Node thisPackage = getPackageNodeFor( packageName );
      packages.remove( thisPackage );
      thisPackage.addOutgoingAssociationsFor( packages );
    }
    catch( Exception ex )
    {
      // ...
    }
}
```

A well-composed method's operations are all at a similar level of abstraction. The first thing that stands out in this method is that after some high-level operations such as *getAllPackageNodesFor*, suddenly it is doing low-level string manipulation at ❶.

The motivation for this manipulation is to pass the correct package name as a parameter at ❷. It turns out that the *getPackageNodeFor* method can be passed the original *fileName*. The string manipulation to construct the package name can be performed at the beginning of that lower-level method. Thus, now the method becomes:

Listing 15.2 An improved composed method.

```
  // BETTER

private void calculateMetrics( String fileName, ZipFile zipFile )
{
    try
    {
      ClassFile file = loader.getClassFileFromZip( fileName, zipFile );
      Collection classes = getAllNonSystemClassesFor( file.getClasses() );
      Collection packages = getAllPackageNodesFor( classes );

❶    Node thisPackage = getPackageNodeFor( fileName ) ;
❷    dependsOnPackages.remove( thisPackage );
❸    thisPackage.addOutgoingAssociationsFor( packages ) ;
```

```
        }
        catch( Exception ex )
        {
            // ...
        }
    }
```

There is still a problem with varying levels of abstraction. The two statements starting at ❶ are not at the same level of abstraction as the prior steps—they are performing low-level collection manipulation.

Statements ❶ and ❷ are preparation for the major statement at ❸ to *addOutgoingAs-
sociationsFor*. It turns out that these lower-level operations can also be moved into a
new helper method *addOutgoingAssociations* that hides the details (and which is
responsible for updating the collection of *Nodes* held by this object).

The final results show a relatively well-composed method. Observe that it is quite
readable—the body of the method does not really require any internal comments.

Listing 15.3 A composed method.

```
// BEST - a Composed Method
private void calculateMetrics( String fileName, ZipFile zipFile )
{
    try
    {
        ClassFile file = loader.getClassFileFromZip( fileName, zipFile );
        Collection classes = getAllNonSystemClassesFor( file.getClasses() );
        Collection packages = getAllPackageNodesFor( classes );
        addOutgoingAssociations( fileName, packages ) ;
    }
    catch( Exception ex )
    {
        // ...
    }
}
```

One last hint in refactoring: If a method shows two or three messages in sequence to another class of object, that is an indication that those messages should be composed into a new method in the other class.

```
  // BETTER, factored

public void enableService()
{
  service.startAndEnable();
}

  // WORSE, un-factored

public void enableService()
{
  service.initialize();
  service.configure();
  service.enable();
}
```

15.2 INTENTION REVEALING MESSAGE

Contrast the following two code examples:

```
if ( isNewSale() )
{
  // ...
}


if ( isAudioEnabled() )
{
  // ...
}
```

```
if ( sale == null )
{
  // ...
}
```

```
if ( Boolean.getBoolean( "sound" ) )
{
  // ...
}
```

The first style is an example of applying the **Intention Revealing Message** coding pattern [Beck 1997]; a helper method wraps a *short* snippet of code. Although these examples are for boolean tests, the pattern can be applied to other kinds of methods. This very fine-grained factoring can be overkill in some cases, but when used it has the following benefits:

■ It more clearly reveals the *intention* for performing the operation and thus enhances readability and comprehension, without the need for comments.

■ It encapsulates a lower level implementation, such as the representation detail that a new sale is signified by a *null* value in an instance field. This allows a change in the representation without breaking the code that sends the intention revealing message.

■ It provides an easy mechanism to extend the logic.

With respect to this last point, it is possible that the test for the state of the sale will evolve. For example:

```
// early version

private boolean isNewSale()
{
  return sale == null;
}
```

```
// later version

private boolean isNewSale()
{
  return sale == null || register.isClear();
}
```

15.3 IMPORT DECLARATIONS

There are two ways to declare imports: **single-type-import** and **type-import-on-demand** [GJS 1996]. Single-type-import declarations, not surprisingly, import a single type. Type-import-on-demand declarations allow the compiler to *find* all public types from a given package on demand.[1] Here is how the two import styles would be used to import the *java.io* classes needed for custom serialization behavior:

```
// BETTER, type-import-on-demand

import java.io.*;

// WORSE, single-type-import

import java.io.IOException;
import java.io.ObjectInputStream;
import java.io.ObjectOutputStream;
import java.io.Serializable;
```

Proponents of single-type-import point to the explicit nature of the import as an advantage. With single-type-import, accidental import of two like-named classes is

---

1. A common confusion with the *import* statement is thinking it is like a C++ *#include* directive; it is not. *import* does not "import" or include code; it simply informs the compiler where to look when resolving type names.

not possible. Both classes must be explicitly imported. They also point to the fact that single-type-import yields information related to class coupling. In practice, neither of these arguments are particularly convincing. As for the first argument, this condition is exceedingly rare. It does happen, but it is trivial to work around (switch to single-type-imports or refer to classes by fully-qualified names). As for the second argument, *reliable* system-level analysis of coupling *cannot* be achieved by human inspection of import statements; it is both error prone and an inefficient way to analyze coupling. The best way to analyze the coupling between types is to buy or write tools designed for that purpose, such as a reverse engineering CASE tool or a type-dependency analyzer program written in Java.[1] Don't rely on import declarations.

On the other hand, type-import-on-demand *does* have significant arguments in its favor; type-import-on-demand declarations are easier to write, easier to read, and easier to maintain. They're easy to write because they require fewer keystrokes. They're easy to read because they are much more compact vertically. (We have seen single-type-import declarations dozens of lines long. How obnoxious!) However, it is the issue of maintenance that really nails the coffin shut for single-type-import. Single-type-import requires the constant back-and-forth of coding, importing, coding, importing. As the class evolves, the imports must be repeatedly changed to reflect the modified coupling. Single-type import is particularly susceptible to human error. If a class changes so that it no longer needs a particular import, but a developer forgets to remove the import, the code will compile, but the visual analysis of class coupling by reading the import statements is now incorrect and misleading.

Liberate yourselves from the tyranny of the single-type-import! Declare your imports with type-import-on-demand and get to coding!

Declare imports with type-import-on-demand.

---

1. The analyzer reads a collection of *.class files, constructs a dependency graph, and prints a report summarizing the coupling. It is simple to write in Java using the Reflection API.

```
import java.util.io.*;
```

Now that the issue of import style has been chosen, how are the imports to be listed? We recommend using alphabetical order for imports, with a blank line between groups of imports from different organizations to indicate functional areas. This helps categorize imports into natural groups.

Declare imports in alphabetical order, with a blank line between imports from different organizations.

```
import com.odi.pse.*;

import com.objectspace.voyager.*;

import java.io.*;
import java.util.*;

import javax.ejb.*;
import javax.naming.*;
```

15.4 CONSTRUCTOR CHAINING

Java allows constructors to be chained. Constructor chaining allows for common initialization code to be factored into a single constructor. For instance, in the following example the second constructor is chained to the first constructor so that the socket initialization code need not be repeated:

```
public Connection( String host, int port ) throws IOException
{
   this.socket = new Socket( host, port );
   this.in = new DataInputStream( socket.getInputStream() );
   this.out = new DataOutputStream( socket.getOutputStream() );
}

public Connection( String host ) throws IOException
{
   this( host, DEFAULT_PORT );
}
```

(Note the use of the *this* keyword in the field assignments. This is an example of 100% style adherence. By always typing *this* in a constructor, even when it is not necessary to resolve the scope, the usage becomes idiomatic. It actually becomes easier to type it than to ask, "Should I type it?")

One restriction on constructor chaining is that if a constructor invokes another constructor, this invocation must be the first statement. In the following example, the second version of the constructor would not compile:

```
/**
 * This version will compile because the constructor invocation is
 * the first statement in the constructor body.
 */
public Connection( String host ) throws IOException
{
   this( host, DEFAULT_PORT ); //OK
   System.out.println( "Connected to " + host + ":" + DEFAULT_PORT );
}

/**
 * This version will not compile because the constructor invocation is
 * not the first statement in the constructor body.
 */
public Connection( String host ) throws IOException
{
   System.out.println( "Connecting to " + host + " using default port.");
   this( host, DEFAULT_PORT ); //Not OK!
   System.out.println( "Connected to " + host + " using default port.");
}
```

Initialization methods are used to avoid this problem. Instance methods can be invoked from any point within the body of the constructor. These methods are naturally named *initialize()*. For example:

```
public Connection( String host, int port ) throws IOException
{
  initialize( host, port );
}

public Connection( String host ) throws IOException
{
  System.out.println( "Connecting to " + host + " using default port." );
  initialize( host, DEFAULT_PORT );
  System.out.println( "Connected" + host + " using default port.");
}

public void initialize( String host, int port ) throws IOException
{
  this.socket = new Socket( host, port );
  this.in = new DataInputStream( socket.getInputStream() );
  this.out = new DataOutputStream( socket.getOutputStream() );
}
```

15.5 INTERNAL FIELD AND JAVABEANS PROPERTY ACCESS

There is a raging debate over whether or not accessors (getters and setters) should be used to access *internal* fields. For instance, if an *Employee* object has a name, should a method on *Employee* access the name directly via the *name* field, or indirectly via a *getName* accessor? Historically, Smalltalk developers are used to always using accessors, and C++ developers are used to not using them—without any trouble. We recommend...wait for it...avoiding accessors for internal field access. If you access a field on another object, you should almost always use accessors. For your own data, access it directly. This is the approach that the Sun programmers of the

JDK have taken. After years of developing software, we have found it is extremely rare that using accessors internally actually pays off. It turns out to be more trouble than it is worth. Of course, if the development team feels strongly about using them, do it—it's not worth a battle.

On the other hand, when accessing a JavaBeans property, even internal access must be through an accessor. This is most important when changing the value. Bound and constrained properties have event-generating code in the setters. If the field is set directly, this event generation is bypassed and listeners are not notified of changes.

> Always access JavaBeans properties through accessors.

```
// BETTER, if this is a JavaBeans property

setEnabled( true );


// WORSE - bypasses event generation logic

isEnabled = true;
```

15.6 INITIALIZE FIELDS WHERE DECLARED

Unlike C++, Java allows fields to be initialized in the declaration. This makes it easier to understand the nature and role of the fields—the reader need only read the declaration line. If the reader has to scan one or more constructors to determine the field value, then the code is unnecessarily complex. Note that some fields cannot be initialized where declared. In such cases we have no choice but to initialize them in a constructor or method.

Lastly, do not initialize a field in the declaration only to turn around and re-initialize it to a constructor parameter value. The original value becomes garbage. .

> When possible, initialize fields where declared unless the field will be re-initialized from a constructor parameter.

```
// BETTER - one line to read

private Collection clients = new ArrayList();

// WORSE - two lines must be read to understand

private Collection clients;

public Server()
{
  this.clients = new ArrayList();
}
```

15.7 STRINGTOKENIZER INSTEAD OF INDEXOF/SUBSTRING

String parsing is commonly performed in many applications. Unfortunately, string parsing is an inherently ugly business: lots of *indexOf, substring*, "off-by-one" errors,

StringIndexOutOfBoundsException, and so forth. The *StringTokenizer* class makes it a bit prettier, and is still quite efficient.

Consider the following manual tokenization:

```
String string = "com.foo.bar";
int begin = 0;
int end = 0;

while ( (end = string.indexOf( ".", begin ) ) != -1 )
{
  System.out.println( string.substring( begin, end ) );
  begin = end + 1;
}

System.out.println( string.substring( begin ) );
```

When run, this code prints:

```
com
foo
bar
```

It works, but it's ugly, complex, and difficult to understand. Here is the *StringTokenizer* code:

```
String string = "com.foo.bar";
StringTokenizer tokens = new StringTokenizer( string, "." );

while( tokens.hasMoreTokens() )
  System.out.println( tokens.nextToken() );
```

No off-by-one errors, no *StringIndexOutOfBoundsException*—trivial to write and understand.

Moral: Use *StringTokenizer* instead of *indexOf/substring* unless there is a compelling reason to do otherwise.

BIBLIOGRAPHY

[ABW 1997] Albert, S., Brown, K., Woolf, B. *The Design Patterns Smalltalk Companion.* Addison-Wesley.

[Beck 1997] Beck, K. *Smalltalk Best Practice Patterns.* Prentice Hall.

[Bloch 1998] Bloch, J. "The Java Tutorial: Collections Trail." http://java.sun.com/docs/books/tutorial/collections/index.html

[BMRSS 1996] Buschman, F., et al. *Pattern Oriented Software Architecture.* John Wiley & Sons.

[Celko 1999] Celko, J. Joe Celko's *SQL for Smarties : Advanced SQL Programming.* Morgan Kaufmann.

[Fowler 1999] Fowler, M. *Refactoring: Improving the Design of Existing Code.* Addison-Wesley. *Not yet published at time of this printing.*

[GHJV 1995] Gamma, E., Helm, R., Johnson, R., and Vlissides, J. 1995. *Design Patterns.* Reading, MA.: Addison-Wesley.

[GJS 1996] Gosling, J., Joy, B., Steele, G. *The Java Language Specification.* Addison-Wesley.

[HM 1998] Hunt, J., and McManus, A. *Key Java: Advanced Tips and Techniques.* Springer-Verlag.

[Jones 1981] Jones, T.C. *Programming Productivity: Issues for the Eighties* (IEEE Catalog No. EHO 186-7).

[Larman 1997] Larman, C. *Applying UML and Patterns—An Introduction to Object-Oriented Analysis and Design*. Prentice Hall.

[Lea 1996] Lea, D. *Concurrent Programming in Java*. Addison-Wesley.

[Lea 1997a] Lea, D. Tutorial notes from OOPSLA 1997 on "Concurrent Programming in Java". ACM Publication.

[Lea 1997b] Lea, D. "Concurrent Programming in Java," Online Supplement http:// gee.cs.oswego.edu/dl/cpj/index.html.

[Martin 1995] Martin, R. *Designing Object-Oriented C++ Applications*. Prentice-Hall.

[Meyer 1988] Meyer, B. *Object-Oriented Software Construction*. Prentice Hall.

[Pearson 1990] Pearson, P. "Fast Hashing of Variable Length Text Strings." *Commun. ACM* 33,6 (June 1990).

[PLOP 1996] ed. Coplien, J., Vlissides, J., and Kerth, N. *Pattern Languages of Program Design 2*. Addison-Wesley.

[PLOP 1997] ed. Buschman, F., Martin, R., Riehle, D. *Pattern Languages of Program Design 3*. Addison-Wesley.

[Uzgalis 1991] Uzgalis, R. "General Hash Functions." TR. 91-01 Computer Science Department, University of Hong Kong, January 1991

[Weiss 1998] Weiss, M. *Data Structures and Algorithm Analysis in Java*. Addison-Wesley.

INDEX

for registration 209
strength reduction 105
String
   efficient search 105
   parsing with StringTokenizer 291
   performance 75, 76, 77, 78
StringBuffer 75, 76, 78
StringTokenizer
   for String parsing 291
subclass
   naming 258
symmetry of equality 119
synchronization
   double-checked locking 100
   of class 154
   of container 171
   using mutex object 156
synchronized-view 171

T

tagging interface 198
terminating thread 161
testing
   Java-specific advice 248
   JUnit 239
   location of testing code 249
   order of 245
   package 248
   realistic 250
   regression testing 246
   test case 240
   test fixture 243
   test suite 242
   testing framework 239
   using Java 2 Reflection features 238
   what not to test 247
   what to test 247
   white-box 238
thread
   exploit idle processor time 42
   scheduling 151
   spawning for method invocation 159
   stack 17
   terminating 161
   use less 45
   use more 45
thread pool 32
thread priority 147, 151
threaded object 160
threadsafe container 171

throwing exception 192
time
   performance-currentTimeMillis 93
toString method 128
type-import-on-demand 285

U

UML
   package diagram 224
unmodifiable view 173

V

value-base equality 116
view definition 168

W

wait method 148
weak typing 85
while loop for guarded suspension 152